O LORD my God,
I called to you for help
and you healed me.

Psalm 30:2

A gift for: _____

From: _____

Healed by His Hands
Copyright © 2007 by Zondervan
ISBN 978-0-310-81204-3

All Scripture quotations, unless otherwise noted, are taken from
the *Holy Bible: New International Version*®. NIV®. (North American Edition)®. Copyright 1973, 1978, 1984 by International Bible Society. Used by
permission of Zondervan. All rights reserved.

The "NIV" and "New International Version" trademarks are registered
in the United States Patent and Trademark Office by International Bible
Society.

Scripture quotations marked NRSV are taken from *The New Revised Standard Version Bible*. Copyright © 1989 by the Division of Christian Education of the National Council of the Churches of Christ in the United
States of America and are used by permission. All rights reserved.

All rights reserved. No part of this publication may be reproduced, stored
in a retrieval system, or transmitted in any form or by any means—electronic, mechanical, photocopy, recording, or any other—except for
brief quotations in printed reviews, without the prior permission of the
publisher.

Requests for information should be addressed to:
Inspirio, the gift group of Zondervan
Grand Rapids, Michigan 49530
www.inspiriogifts.com

Project Manager: Kim Zeilstra
Writing and Compilation: Manuscript was written by Deborah Kaye
    Webb in association with SnapdragonGroup℠ Editorial Services
Production Manager: Matt Nolan
Design Manager: Michael J. Williams
Design: Jay Smith, Juicebox Designs
Cover and Interior Illustrations: Jody Williams

Printed in China
07 08 09 / 4 3 2 1

Healed
by his hands

Biblical Stories of Those Touched by the Son of God

Deborah Kaye Webb

inspirio®

Foreword

Out of a small town in the northern region of Israel, Jesus came preaching a message of hope and healing. The common folks welcomed him with open arms. And why wouldn't they? Traveling from one city to the next, Jesus touched their broken lives—one fractured person after another—restoring sight to the blind, hearing to the deaf, speech to the mute, and strength to the lame. He cured all types of illnesses: fever, palsy, epilepsy, leprosy, hemorrhaging, and dropsy. He mended withered limbs, straightened bent backs, and even reattached the severed ear of an enemy. Multitudes followed him, amazed at his power to heal; drawn, as well, to the compelling tenderness they experienced in his presence.

Yet Jesus addressed more than merely physical illness. Just as Isaiah had prophesied, he released those who had been taken captive by evil. He set men and women and children and foreigners free from demons, mental illness, and despair. Those plagued with evil spirits found him always approachable, but the minions of darkness fled in terror at the sound of his voice.

Most profound was the diligence with which Jesus tended to the hearts of those whom he touched. Speaking a message of forgiveness, mercy, and grace, he set at liberty those who were tortured and oppressed by guilt. Prostitutes, thieves, and liars alike found help in Jesus' presence, healing in Jesus' words, and hope in Jesus' saving grace.

Whatever the infirmity, Jesus healed—moment by moment, touch by tender touch—until at last his healing ministry became a threat to the powerful religious regime of his day. Incensed over his unconventional intimacy with the Almighty, his untraditional approach to the sacred Law, and his unwillingness to conform to the status quo, the religious ruling council of his day determined that he must die before their influence and empire came to naught.

In his final and most profound act of healing, Jesus willingly submitted to death by execution in order to heal the breach between God and man.

It is our hope that the healing hands of Jesus will reach through the pages of this book, effectively touching your heart and life, drawing you ever nearer to the one who still holds the cure to all of mankind's infirmity—heart, soul, and mind.

May the healing grace of Jesus continue through the compassionate hearts and faithful prayers of his followers until the day he returns.

> I will heal my people and will let them
> enjoy abundant peace and security.
>
> Jeremiah 33:6

Contents

Introduction 7

The Crippled Lamb at the Sheep Gate..8
(John 5:1–15)

He Carried Our Diseases... 18
(Matthew 8:14–17; Mark 1:29–34; Luke 4:38–41)

The Leper Lover 34
(Matthew 8:1–4; Mark 1:40–45; Luke 5:12–16)

The Faith of Four Friends 46
(Matthew 9:1–7; Mark 2:1–12; Luke 5:17–25)

Son Rise.. 60
(Luke 7:11–17)

The Champion of Death and Dying 69
(Matthew 9:18–26; Mark 5:21–43; Luke 8:40–56)

The Withered Hand Made Whole 82
(Matthew 12:1–14; Mark 2:23–3:6; Luke 6:1–11)

Healing in the Valley of Humiliation... 92
(Matthew 17:9–21; Mark 9:2–29; Luke 9:37–43)

"I Can See!".. 102
(John 9)

Gratitude: God's Reign within the Heart.................................. 111
(Luke 17:11–19)

The Last Lamp Lit 116
(Mark 10:46–52)

The Mission Continues 119
(Acts 3:1–16)

Intro

Though the author considers herself a storyteller by nature, neither she nor anyone else she knows can tell a better story than those recorded in the Bible. They have stood the test of time, bringing home the good news of God's love and grace for centuries. But by adding color in and around the scriptural text, she has attempted to give new clarity to accounts of those touched and healed by Jesus during his ministry here on earth.

In the interest of preserving the absolute and central truths of Scripture—around which the following short stories pivot—the publisher would recommend that the reader first peruse the biblical rendition of each scenario. It will then become obvious wherein the author has used her "sanctified imagination" to fill in the margins—those gaps in the text that were left open—to weave a vivid thread of invention into the text.

The Crippled Lamb at the Sheep Gate

John 5:1 – 15

"I found him," the man reported back to the religious authorities at the temple. "His name is Jesus."

Suspicious glances darted about the hall—ricocheting from one man's eyes to another. "That is precisely what we expected to hear," the elderly councilman said as he folded his arms across his chest. Looking down his nose with a sneer, he continued, "That's all we need from you."

"Wait!" A younger official stepped into the man's path as he turned to leave. "Do you clearly understand the consequences you will face if you are ever again seen carrying your burden on the Sabbath?"

"I understand the consequences," he answered with a slight elevation of his chin. "I just don't understand your reasoning."

The man in authority rapped the floor loudly with his staff. "Are we to assume by your answer that you consider yourself worthy of challenging the High Council?"

"No, I'm certainly not worthy." He turned to face the older man again. "Never claimed to be; but the man who healed me *told* me to pick up my mat and go home."

"The Sabbath tradition strictly forbids a man to carry such a load," he announced sternly. "And the man in question does not have the authority to tell you otherwise."

"It seems to me that his having the power to heal a lame man is proof that he has greater authority than anyone on your Council can lay claim to." His eyes scoured their faces.

"Get him out of here," the younger official barked over his

shoulder at the temple guard.

Exiting the temple, the man glanced toward the Sheep Gate where the pool was located. Strange to think that he might never return there, having spent endless days and sleepless nights lying under those porches—for years—hoping for a miracle.

Was it really hope that had kept him there? Perhaps it was the fellowship of misery. And suddenly, that fellowship was gone.

It seemed surreal to him now. The Sabbath had started like every other. He had lain at the water's edge among a fevered multitude—each taking their turn moaning, wailing, and cursing into the air. Because it was late in the summer, the crippled man had spent the night on one of the porches. All of the disabled—the lame, the blind, the lepers, the epileptics—slept crowded under the five arches overhead. The stench of disease combined with human excrement seemed worse at night, trapped as it was under the shelter. They were accustomed to the smell. But had any tourists stumbled into the infected arena, they would have become immediately aware, by the foulness of the air, that they had wandered from the land of the living.

The legend that had drawn these outcasts to the pool rumored an intermittent stirring of the waters by an angel. The story was that the first one to plunge into the bubbling waters would be healed. In all these years, though, he had never witnessed it. Oh, the waters stirred—yes, regularly. But never so much as a scratch was mended, much less the throng of broken hearts. In any case, the greedy clamor of desperation drove them recklessly into the water by the dozens; and how would anyone know who had made it in first, even with the eyes of an angel?

Even so, there was no one to help him in … not before the others.

Around midmorning, he had lapsed into his routine journey of the mind through the past—remembering the first time he had come to the pool. His mother—weary of the demands of his condition—had finally lost patience with him. One time too many, he had upbraided her for not helping him off his cot soon enough to suit him, and she shouted back in frustration, "Just go to the Pool of Bethesda and try your luck there." That was thirty-three years ago, and his mother had long since died.

Observing a man walking onto the porch, his mind rushed back into the present.

"Are you lost?" he asked.

"No." Jesus shook his head, looking around at the beleaguered crowd of people.

"What, then?" he asked again. "Are you looking for someone?"

"Not really," Jesus answered, still surveying the helpless multitude.

"Just morbid curiosity, huh?"

Jesus turned to look him in the eye.

The cripple shifted under the man's searching glance. "No? Then why are you here? You don't look like you need a miracle."

No answer. Jesus stood in quiet contemplation, his hands clasped loosely in front of him. He had ventured out of the temple because the atmosphere inside was suffocating: the stiff, prestigious robes of the academia; the pretentious, scholarly paraphernalia dangling from their religious garb; the endless and empty debates over Sabbath rules and regulations. Hadn't they read the Scriptures for themselves? Weren't they the experts in the Law?

God blessed the seventh day and declared it holy, because it was the day when he rested from all his work.

The severity of their Sabbath traditions—the imposition of laws so crystallized, men had to walk as if on eggshells to keep from breaking them; the restrictions so binding that they cut off the circulation of the Spirit—this was anything but a rest for God's people. It was more like a test—a test that the crude commoners were destined to fail. The interpretation of the Sabbath by the religious elite had perverted the compassionate intent of the Almighty. What he had meant to be a blessing, they had turned into a curse.

While "holy" men in "high" places sat arguing the intricacies of their religion and trumpeting their superior understanding, the ignorant, suffering citizens entrusted to their care were strewn helplessly around an impotent body of water, lifting *unholy* hands to the heavens, crying out for deliverance, pleading for help, looking to an unnamed angel who was nothing more than the phantom of some long-forsaken hope.

Not one of the self-acclaimed dignitaries would lift so much as a finger to relieve the burden of these poor souls. They were too concerned with impressing each other. Their long-winded, lofty orations sounded to Jesus like the clanging of noisy cymbals—ringing in his ears with the hollow sound of indifference. He had needed to slip away, out into the fresh autumn air, away from the stifling atmosphere of religion, which had hardened within the savage hearts of men who knew no mercy.

Still searching the eyes of the cripple, Jesus spoke at last, "Do you want to get well?"

"I can't, sir." The man wagged his head at the futility of the suggestion. The thought crossed his mind that this able-bodied man might intend to hoist him up into his arms and heave him into the waters at the least ripple of movement.

Silence. The question hung in the air between them, begging an adequate answer.

"I have no one to carry me into the pool when the angel stirs it," he hurried to explain further.

More silence. Quieter than before.

"Perhaps you aren't aware," the lame man continued, "that once the waters are stirred, only the first person into the pool will be healed; someone else always gets there ahead of me." He was straining against the silence, wrestling with a response that offered no answer.

"Do you want to get well?" Jesus asked again.

An uneasy frown creased the man's brow. He could recall that at first he had wanted to get well—many years ago. But he had long since established his identity as a victim of renown—the highly acclaimed veteran of disease. He had seniority here, for no one had occupied the porches longer than he. And he knew them all—their diseases, their sins, their hopes, and their sorrows—as the initiation of every newcomer found them each confessing to this seasoned sufferer.

But he couldn't admit that to the stranger, so he simply said, "I'm here, aren't I?"

"Stand up!" Jesus calmly commanded.

"What?" His eyes widened with surprise.

"Stand up!" He motioned with his hand for the lame man to rise to his feet. "Pick up your mat and walk away from this."

That was the moment he felt it—the searing sensation of

strength coursing down his spine and into his legs. He sprang up from the ground, staring down at his limbs as if seeing them for the first time.

"What the—?"

His neighbors gasped: "What is going on?" "Who is that man?" "What did he say to you?"

Stunned and bewildered, the man rolled up his mat and made his way off the porch. As he headed into town, trying to determine what he should do, he encountered two rabbis on their way to the temple.

"What do you think you're doing?" one of them scolded, stopping him on the street.

"I'm walking home." The words felt strange in his mouth. Having spent most of his life as an invalid, he had never dared dream he would walk again. Perhaps he and the Healer should have discussed this before. After all, a man might want to count the cost of deliverance before agreeing to it.

"You can't work on the Sabbath, you fool!" the other shouted. "Drop that bundle immediately and come with us."

That was how it had happened. That was how he had come into the temple courts to face the Council.

"Why were you carrying your mat?" The accusation shot from the old councilman's lips with unmistakable aim.

"The man who healed me told me to."

"What do you mean, speaking such nonsense? Explain yourself."

"I've been crippled for thirty-eight years. You know it is true, you've seen me yourself at the temple gate, begging alms. It is my custom on the Sabbath to go to the Sheep Gate and wait for the angel to stir the waters. But today, a stranger appeared among us, and he healed me."

"Why you? You are a sinner," the younger official cut in.

"I don't know why." He felt indignation rising in his chest. In the face of his deliverance, how could they be so indifferent as to be concerned only about their rules—sensing no triumph in his healing? "Do you think it's possible that the mercy of God is indiscriminate, after all?"

"That's enough, you fool!" the older man admonished.

"Perhaps you mean to agree, then, that the love of God is meant for fools; for there is no denying that I've been healed by a power greater than yours."

"Get out!" the councilman shouted. "And when you discover who did this unconscionable deed on a holy day, you are to report back to us immediately. Do you understand?"

"I'm afraid I do," he murmured as he walked away. "You have condemned a man for committing a scandalous act of kindness on a day you had set aside for your own glory."

Once more he exited the temple. This time he left by the eastern gate, the one they called Beautiful. He paused under the richly ornamented arches—feasting his eyes on the dazzling Corinthian brass, and then following the terraced platform to the twelve easy steps, once insurmountable to the cripple.

This was the holy mound that true-hearted Israelites had ascended for ages, worshiping the Creator of their able bodies, the Sovereign of their noblest hopes. Suddenly he felt the unfamiliar stab of conscience. How could he—now an able-bodied Israelite—descend those same stairs with a false heart ... having failed to acknowledge the compassion of his Sovereign Lord? Turning again, he stood humbly upon the threshold of a new hope—a life restored.

Some people cling to their weaknesses. Staking their reputation on being victimized, they think suffering justifies their bitterness, insolence, and lack of initiative. Yet they gather with those who truly seek deliverance at the wellspring of hope, thinking to conceal their charade. But Jesus sees ... and Jesus knows.

Other people oppress those who suffer. Staking their claim to power on the vulnerabilities of the weak, they always appear in religious circles, justifying acts of indifference against the innocent, the unsuspecting, and the meek. Wearing the thin veneer of righteousness, they pretend to be defenders of the faith. Yet Jesus sees ... and Jesus knows.

Seizing upon a ripe moment, the Healer moves on behalf of some unworthy soul, setting the inevitable confrontation into motion: one man coming to grips with his own sinful heart and one religious movement coming to terms with the heart of the Holy One.

He Carried Our Diseases

Matthew 8:14 – 17; Mark 1:29 – 34;
Luke 4:38 – 41

The curtain finally fell on the Sabbath as the sun surrendered and faded into the horizon. It had been a long, eventful day.

Pacing the earthen floor, Haskell had waited—watching out the window for the sun's descent—while Jemina's condition worsened with each passing hour. He couldn't risk being seen carrying her out into the streets in broad daylight. The synagogue would frown on a Sabbath violation such as that. A devout man can't carry a burden any heavier than an egg. Had his donkey fallen into a pit or had his ox stumbled into a ravine, anyone would have understood the necessity of coming to its aid. But according to the priesthood and the Pharisees, human illness must be suffered on the Sabbath and healing sought only when the holy day has ended—at sunset.

Haskell had never been in the habit of questioning the rabbinical ordinances or authorities … that is, until now—now that his Jemina lay dying of a scorching fever. All of a sudden, in light of his wife's crisis, none of it made any sense. Would the Almighty wink at the rescue of a brute beast while condemning such an attempt on behalf of a human, the most glorious creature in his dominion? The battle in his mind raged on.

Added to the feelings of futility was the controversy that surrounded the Rabbi from Nazareth who had spoken at synagogue that morning. Though no official position had been handed down yet from Jerusalem, it had been rumored that the leaders were frowning at his perceived disregard for their long-cherished traditions. Never mind that the details added by their meticulous interpretations weren't actually prescribed in the Law of Moses. They claimed that God had entrusted the law to the likes of them—educated men—who were commissioned to translate it to the crude masses of common Jews ... like Haskell. Come to think of it, Haskell had always harbored a nagging suspicion that the God he worshipped didn't necessarily consider it a compliment to be represented by the self-righteous men who went about announcing their superior spiritual status by wearing ridiculously garnished robes.

In any case, the Sabbath was finally over and Jemina had survived, though barely. The old man turned in haste from the window and hurried to wrap his fevered wife into his mantle, lifting her from her cot. He caught a stale whiff of her sweat-soaked pallet and grimaced. Straining with every ounce of his strength, he raised her into his embrace and stood upright, grunting aloud.

It hadn't been this difficult forty-three years ago when he carried her over the threshold of his father's house and into the room he had built for their wedded bliss. Now, in his old age, every step was a labor of love. Even so, the stooped, gray-bearded Hebrew set one foot heavily in front of the other as he made his way out of the dwelling and into the streets of Capernaum.

"Look, it's old Haskell," the whispering began at the doorstep of his next-door neighbor. "Where do you think he's taking Jemina?"

"Haskell," her head rolled toward him on the ball of his

shoulder and he felt her searing lips touch his ear. "Where are we going?"

"Shhh, Jemina," he panted heavily, concentrating on the effort of walking. He didn't have strength to talk.

"But it's getting dark," she whispered faintly.

Haskell felt tears sting his sockets. He certainly hadn't intended to put her in this situation—making her vulnerable to her worst fears. Jemina had always had a peculiar fear of twilight. Haskell had always been suspicious that the lengthening shadows of the evening played upon her imagination as if they were demons darting about. But she wouldn't talk to him about it, neither to confirm nor to refute his impressions. She simply took measures to brace herself against the daily haunt, insisting that the children be safe inside the dwelling before the sun set and occupying herself with her domestic responsibilities. It had appeared to him that her many efforts to avoid the threat of evil were effective enough to stall until the night settled in, calming her anxiety while the gentle moonlight bathed the darkening sky as a backdrop to the twinkling consolation of the stars.

I hope I'm right about the Rabbi's whereabouts, Haskell turned his fretting toward his own anxiety on this particular twilight. He had guessed that the Teacher would be staying with one of the fishermen—Peter or Andrew. Jesus' hometown of Nazareth would have been an impossible destination for a Sabbath night's journey, having only a little daylight remaining once the sun had set. Besides, he had heard that Jesus hadn't resumed his residence in Nazareth. It seemed he had finished with his carpenter's shop. And no reasonable man would question his decision. Nothing good ever came out of Nazareth.

As he approached the hilly road that led up to the houses of the fishermen, he became certain that his guess was accurate.

There, ahead of him, were dozens of other people making their way to Simon Peter's dwelling. Several individuals walked alone, but then clusters of people came dragging lame relatives on cots or carrying  crippled friends propped between two sets of shoulders. Haskell recognized that these people had reasoned, just as he had, that there might be a chance that the Teacher would use his authority to fight the ravages of illness, as he had the demons earlier in the day.

Haskell stopped and lowered Jemina to the ground, easing himself down under her frail body to cushion her from the damp sod. He simply had to stop before attempting that climb. It looked like a formidable barrier at the moment. It would take all of his stamina to get her to the crest of it—that is, if he made it at all.

Somewhat disheartened that half the town had turned out ahead of him to beg similar favors, he bowed his face into Jemina's headcovering and prayed sofly: "Adonai, hear the humble petition of one who is unworthy of heaven's favor. I hold to my bosom the dearest thing on earth to me and dearer still to thee. I have taken care to protect and provide for her until this very day, though at times with halting steps. But now, I have met a foe against whom I am powerless—a burning fever that threatens to snatch the breath of life right out of her lungs. O God of heaven, please hear! On behalf of one you love—far more deserving than I—give me the strength to climb this hill and get her to the Rabbi who I believe possesses your power to heal … in spite of what the authorities say about him. Amen."

The tears that had welled up earlier now spilled freely onto the fabric of Jemina's shawl. *There's no time for such weakness*, he scolded himself, rising back to his feet with his wife in tow.

"Cale!" He startled, though at the sound of a familiar voice. "That's old Haskell coming. Go fetch Jemina from him before he falls flat on his face!"

"Mika," Jemina roused slightly in recognition.

Mika was Jemina's first cousin who lived only a short distance away. She and Jemina had always been close, though Mika was considerably younger. Mika had trained as a midwife under the renowned Shara from Bethany and had gained quite a reputation for always being where people needed her. Having no children of her own, she had devoted her life to the nurturing of others.

Mika's husband, Cale—a strong ox of a man—advanced toward Haskell with a loping gait. Sweeping Jemina out of the old man's arms, he carried her in his solid embrace as if she were merely a sack of husks. Making his way to Mika, he stood holding Jemina, waiting for instructions about what to do next.

"Just lay her on this cot, here." Mika pointed to the place she had prepared for Cale and Jemina to sit and wait.

"So you heard, did you?" Mika seized Haskell's elbow to assist, as he staggered the few remaining steps uphill.

"Heard what?" he puffed, his heart fairly pounding in his chest, echoing in his ears like a drum beating out a dirge. *I hope I don't die myself, now that I've made it here with Jemina*, he thought in passing.

"About Natania! What else?" Mika's eyes widened with surprise.

Natania was Peter's mother-in-law, who lived with him and his wife.

"What are you talking about?" Haskell squatted down beside

Jemina, reaching to secure the mantle about her shoulders.

"Haskell, where have you been?" Mika smacked the heel of her hand to her forehead in exasperation. "This has been a day of signs and wonders in Israel—a day the likes of which men have not gazed upon since the days of Elijah!"

"You mean the happenings at synagogue," he nodded. "I was there!"

"No! Yes!" She pounded her fist into her palm. "I mean, no! That was only the beginning!"

"What then?"

"The incident with Natania!"

"What about her?" Haskell was confused. "Are all these people here to see Natania?"

Everyone knew Natania, though not because of Peter. She had her own reputation. A beautiful woman with dark, expressive eyes, Natania was fiery tempered and sharp tongued. Natania knew everyone in Capernaum as well as everyone's private affairs. She made it her primary occupation to know everyone else's business, and she was the mill from which a majority of the local gossip was ground. If you wanted to know, you wanted to know Natania's spin on the matter. Anything less was considered unauthorized and unworthy of repeating.

Mika's eyes glistened in the soft glow of the early moonlight. She relished the opportunity to break fresh news.

"After that scene at synagogue, Cale and I hung around waiting to extend an invitation to the demonized man—it being the Sabbath and all," she began, savoring every word. "There were several others, too, who lingered in the aftermath of the exorcism, just too stunned to resume the routine matters of the day, I suppose."

"I found it difficult myself, but Jemina was home sick," Haskell responded, wishing he could have been among those who stayed.

"In the middle of our meal, my brother David burst into the house and announced, 'Word has it that Natania is burning up with the fever of plague!'"

Haskell gasped. "No! Not Natania."

"It's a fact," Mika nodded emphatically, pleased with Haskell's appalled reaction. "I flew to my feet and ran as far as the Sabbath would allow, stopping at the market square. I was not alone—there were several of us present. I overheard one woman say to her daughter while we waited for a report, 'Let this teach you what happens to those who set the world aflame with blazing tongues; they are set on fire themselves!'

"By and by, Natania's niece came running down the hill shouting, 'She's well! It's a miracle! The Rabbi healed her!'"

"Healed her! Tell me more, Mika. I need details."

"Be patient, old man, I'm telling you as fast as I can remember it!" Mika leaned across Haskell to feel Jemina's forehead with her hand, offering a slight delay in a mild resistance to his pressure. "Well, it seems that Natania and Marité, Peter's wife, had returned from synagogue early, making preparations for the Sabbath meal, since they were hosting the new Rabbi. Jesus, Peter, Andrew, James, and John had been detained. About an hour prior to their arrival, according to Marité's report, Natania suddenly gasped, fainted, and collapsed onto the floor. Marité rushed to her mother's side and discovered that she was running a very high fever.

"Upon the return of the men, Marité ran to Peter in tears, notifying him of the peculiar happenstance. Only moments before, Natania had been fine. Suddenly, she was delirious and appeared to be in great peril.

"Peter, of course, turned to Jesus, 'Rabbi, I haven't been privileged to witness a healing miracle with my own eyes, but I have seen enough evidence to be convinced of your power. Please take note of my wife's mother.'

"At that, Jesus walked immediately to the cot where she lay, stood over her a moment, frowning in contemplation; then with an authoritative voice he rebuked her fever, 'Be gone!'

"Peter and Andrew exchanged troubled glances.

"Then the Teacher bent over her and put his hand on her forehead. She opened her eyes and stared at him, blinking, apparently from disbelief. Taking her by the hand, Jesus raised her up from the mat. She appeared to be affected as one who had been delivered from great peril. She bowed quietly, kissing the Rabbi's hand out of gratitude, and went right to work preparing the meal as if nothing had ever happened."

"Is that it?" Haskell felt so out of touch; he wanted to make certain there wasn't anything else he had missed.

"Word has it that Natania prepared a meal for the Rabbi fit for a king!" Mika's excitement had begun to wane. "So tell me about Jemina. Is she worse?"

"That's why I'm here," Haskell nodded. "It never occurred to me, though, that others would have the same thought."

"The whole town has heard about the healing miracle by now." Mika's eyes surveyed the crowd. "What do you think the Nazarene will do?"

As if on cue, a hush hurried through the hopeful throng.

Peter shouted from the doorway, "The Rabbi has retired for the evening. Please return to your homes and …"

Suddenly, the Teacher appeared behind Peter's shoulder, placing a hand on him to halt his words. He spoke, but quietly, to Peter alone. Someone nearby overheard it and sent the message back through the crowd: "Friend," he had said, "we must not send them away like this. They need help."

At that, Jesus passed through the door and into the crowd, reaching out to receive the earliest arrival—a babe in arms, wrapped in his mother's tearful embrace. Haskell strained through the twilight to watch with wonder as a look of tenderness fell over the Rabbi's face and onto the child. *Who is this man?* he wondered.

The next morning, Jemina was awake before dawn. "Haskell," she whispered.

He stirred and rolled over to face her, relieved that she was still with him.

"I dreamed that the Rabbi healed me," she continued talking, though quietly.

"Jemina, my dear," Haskell reached to touch her face. "That was not a dream."

"You should have been there!" she rattled on, excited by the awakening of her memory. "I opened my eyes and there he was, his hand on your shoulder, nodding his head, listening to something you were saying, frowning with concern. Suddenly, he knelt onto my pallet and raised me up into his arms. I felt my head resting in the crook of his elbow. His cloak was cool against my burning skin. He smoothed my hair away from my face and, I swear it, Haskell, I have never felt hands as gentle as his."

With his aging vision, Haskell could not make out the smile on Jemina's face, though his ears could so readily discern it.

He listened patiently as Jemina finished telling her dream. "The Teacher then lifted his gaze to the heavens and said simply, 'Abba, look upon this dear woman, as well, and let your compassion move over her ailing frame with healing ...'"

"Jemina," Haskell said as he wiped moisture from his eyes with the back of his hand. "It wasn't a dream, my dear."

"What?" She sat up.

"You weren't dreaming, you were just delirious from fever." Haskell rested his hand on her back. "Don't you remember walking home with me in the middle of the night?"

"Yes, but I thought that was part of my dream." She turned her head to look into her husband's eyes, searching for evidence of his habit of teasing her.

"Many people were healed last night, Jemina," he continued soberly.

"Really?"

"I saw things I never imagined ..." His words trailed off into the soulful silence of contemplation.

"What?"

"Well, how long has old Itzak been crippled?"

"I'd say at least twenty years," she guessed. "Maybe twenty-two." Jemina prided herself in remembering the details of people's lives. It made them feel important and cared for.

"He's not crippled anymore!"

"What?" Jemina twisted her whole body around to face Haskell.

"He's as strong as an ox."

"You shouldn't tease an old woman," Jemina punched gently at his chest.

"I'll take you over there as soon as the sun's up, and you can see for yourself," Haskell smiled.

"What else?"

"We'll just take a stroll through the neighborhood this morning, Jemina, and then you can see what amazing things have happened here."

"I'm really well, aren't I? No coughing, no weakness, nothing."

"That's about all there is to say." Haskell stroked Jemina's arm lovingly.

"Did I hear something about Natania?" Jemina tilted her head slightly, as if attempting to tip something loose from her memory.

"She's fine, I assure you," Haskell laughed softly.

"So she's not in any danger now?" Jemina's genuine love for people knotted up on her brow.

"No, the Teacher delivered her from her wicked visitor and her wicked tongue all in one moment." He grinned at Jemina and winked.

"You should be ashamed, old man." Jemina gave Haskell's beard a gentle tug. "You might want to put a watch on your own tongue."

Haskell reached with his arms, inviting Jemina into his early morning embrace. "Jemina," he looked wistfully up into the darkness above him.

"What is it, my dear?" Jemina nestled into his chest, her head resting against his shoulder.

"I noticed the most peculiar thing."

"What?"

"While the young Rabbi was making his way through the crowd last night, he touched every single person he healed."

"He's very compassionate, isn't he? Not like the other rabbis."

"Yeah, but that's not my point."

"What, then?"

"It was the look on his face when he touched them ..." Haskell's voice trailed off as he reached deep into his mind for just the right words.

"What, Haskell? Don't keep me hanging."

"Well, with every act of healing, I observed a pained expression clouding his countenance, but ever so slight. You had to really watch for it; his compassion sort of kept it concealed."

"What do you make of it, Haskell?"

"I don't know, but while I was watching him at such close range, my mind suddenly recalled the prophecy that he himself read in synagogue yesterday."

"Which one?"

"It was from Isaiah: 'Surely our sickness he himself bore and our pains he carried.'"

"He read that yesterday?"

"He did," Haskell sighed, then gave voice to his most profound observation in a mere whisper—as if the dusty old earth couldn't be trusted with such sacred secrets—"I think he did more than merely read those words. I think he fulfilled them."

Just as the Redeemer more than symbolically took away the sins of the world, so did the Healer more than magically cure the diseases that afflict the human race. The suffering Son of God bore in his body not only the punishment for disobedience, but all the dreadful effects that evil had imposed upon this world.

The Leper Lover

Matthew 8:1 – 4; Mark 1:40 – 45;
Luke 5:12 –16

"Lord Caiaphas, I think you should see this letter." The scribe ran breathlessly into the Council's chambers on the east side of the temple court. "It is from a synagogue leader in Galilee."

"The seal has been broken," Caiaphas scowled.

"The priest on duty opened it."

"Who is the letter from?"

"A man brought it in to him just minutes ago."

"What man?"

"Just read the letter, sir. It will all become clear."

Ravid, Ruler of the Synagogue of Chorazin in the northern region of Galilee, to the Officiating Priest in the Holy Temple at Jerusalem:

Shalom. May the mercies of God visit you on the day you receive this correspondence, written by my own hand.

Two days have come and gone since the drama passed just outside our city gates—that concerning a common leper and an uncommon rabbi, one Jesus of Nazareth. No doubt you have already received word of the excitement that the incident has caused in our region. I myself have been so preoccupied with the tumult that I haven't had time to attempt this correspondence before the present moment, neither would I have been able to secure the services of a courier, as it seems that all have turned their attention to the Nazarene—the very one about whom the Council sent notice just weeks ago.

This unconventional teacher cannot even make his way into the city any longer, so surrounded is he by throngs of people, both locally and from every outlying region. He stays out in the open spaces where his audience can swell at will.

Aware of your recently issued precaution concerning his actions and words, I hope to effectively address some of the more perplexing issues regarding these events as they act-ually occurred.

First of all, for the record, permit me to state that I myself have incurred no guilt in the situation, as I have been conscientiously guarding our synagogue services, just as I was instructed by the Sanhedrin Council. As is our custom, neither have I ever allowed a leper inside the house of worship. In fact, you will be happy to note that it is the practice of our own Rabbi Ben Ari to cast stones at the lepers who inhabit the colony between here and Capernaum, ensuring that they do not violate the distance requirement of four cubits from ceremonially clean individuals. Our own devout rabbi increased this distance to eight cubits of his own free will due to the extent of his piety.

I am happy to point out that my jurisdiction was not compromised in regard to Sabbath observances, for this occurrence did not transpire on a Sabbath. Needless to say, I cannot be responsible for the activities of the Nazarene once he is outside the synagogue, much less, outside the city gates.

According to Tameas, a local fisherman, the rabbi in question—this man, Jesus—had been seen in the predawn hours, climbing a hill just outside Capernaum, having stayed the night at the house of Simon Peter, also a fisherman belonging to the *company of Zebedee in Bethsaida.*

On that particular night, after the Sabbath ended, nearly the entire city of Capernaum had thronged the house of Simon Peter looking for the Nazarene. Rumor has it that he had successfully exorcised a demon from a man in their synagogue, albeit during the proceedings of worship on the holy day, thereby disturbing the decorum of the synagogue service.

You yourselves are well-acquainted with the vulgar impulses of common people who, in their ignorance, flock to every self-proclaimed prophet or zealot promising social reform or liberation from Rome. I hasten to add, so as to save you from any unnecessary embarrassment were you to confront him, that this Jesus doesn't himself engage in such bold self-proclamation, but is given to insisting that the kingdom is about to be reinstated, thereby merely insinuating that he is the catalyst for a monumental overturn. Oddly, he has enlisted the support of some very unimpressive men in our region who, like him, have neither official schooling nor authorization from the rabbinical order that would qualify them to lead such an uprising.

Tameas—also a friend of Peter's brother, Andrew—inquired about the rabbi's suspicious departure from the house of Peter. According to Andrew, he had vacated the premises in the predawn hours in order to pray, having spent the night allegedly working miracles of healing. The brothers were themselves sleeping, having been exhausted from the day's events.

Hordes of people arose early that next morning looking for the Healer, but he was not to be found; that is, until Simon Peter and Andrew tracked him into the hills where, as I said, he was discovered bending the knee in heavenly address.

The news of the mass healing reached Chorazin almost as early as the sun, causing quite a stir inside our city, as well. Since the Sabbath was past, I set out to research the facts of the situation, going on foot the short distance to Capernaum to speak with Jairus, one of the respected synagogue officials in that city. Having arrived in the late morning, I discovered that Rabbi Jesus had proceeded from the hillside where he had been found praying and was headed toward Chorazin from a more northerly route than my own journey had taken me.

Anxious to return and hoping to catch sight of him, I took a moment to confirm the account of exorcism, since it had happened under Jairus's jurisdiction. Jairus was nervous about the inquiry, hoping to be absolved of any blame or alleged support of the breach of our revered Law. Confirm, he did. The man was healed right before his eyes.

Having received a satisfactory account of the Sabbath's events, I hurried to return to Chorazin.

Just as I approached the city gates, I saw a multitude of people making their way out of the city. The overriding tenor of their mood could best be described as that in the amphitheatre once the lion has been lanced. Their faces were alight with an ecstatic anticipation of what might happen next.

The Nazarene was coming down the northwesterly pass, between the two hills, when suddenly one of the lepers from the colony broke from his fellows and ran—though limping severely—right up to him.

There is no need to inquire whether the leper violated the four-cubit rule. I assure you, he did, falling to his feeble knees right at the rabbi's feet, crying out, "Lord!"

Now obviously, there is not another rabbi who has earned the shameful reputation of being so approachable that a filthy leper would dare to run to him for sanctuary. I might as well say it: It was the picture of a vile sinner presuming to defile the sanctified presence of a holy man.

Furthermore, no respectable rabbi would have allowed such vulgar and insulting behavior, but would have instead struck the leper with his staff and spat upon him, thereafter immediately reporting him to the local authorities, sanctioning disciplinary actions befitting his crime.

I continued advancing toward the scene and was well within earshot as the words of the leper fell upon the rabbi's hearing: "If you are willing to do so, I know that you can make me clean."

Permit me to take pause here to describe the state of his uncleanness, as I was now within close, yet lawful, range, witnessing the encounter as it unfolded right before my eyes. This man was full of leprosy. There wasn't so much as a bare patch of clean skin on his face, and his teeth were few and decaying, dangling from raw and inflamed gums. His scalp was also covered with sores and peppered with oozing scabs, matting the thin, yellowing hair that sparsely covered his head. The flesh of his hands and feet were likewise consumed with the disease. Several *of his fingers were stubbed and there were deep, infected craters in the flesh where a man's knuckles should have protruded. His toenails, where still attached, had the look of camel's hoofs, dark and thick, surrounded by swelling. And though he did not touch Jesus, the smell of his rotting flesh was enough to stop a man, assaulting the nostrils with a noxious aroma.*

And though I was appalled at the behavior of this crude sinner, that atrocity paled in comparison to the teacher's response.

I regret to be the bearer of this unthinkable insult as it reflects on the order of priests, rabbis, and all who esteem themselves learned and set apart for strict observance of the law, but it simply must be reported: The rabbi's countenance immediately melted into a look of unrestrained pity, his eyes swimming, as it were, in deep pools of compassion; and before I could find my voice, thinking to shout him to his senses, he reached out with his bare hand and laid his palm right atop the man's loathsome head.

Needless to say, I gasped in horror—now incapable of holding back my disgust—and exclaimed, "What are you thinking?"

He never even heard me, so engrossed was the teacher in the man's revolting condition. His words spoke to the man's request for cleansing. Bending over the leper, as his hand made contact, he very quietly uttered the words: "I am willing!"

I could not determine in the moment whether it was a condition of utter shock and dismay, but I thought I saw his skin instantly healing over. I blinked and rubbed my eyes, suspicious that I was simply staggered at the appalling behavior I had witnessed. But straining for a better look and standing at only the distance of a man's height, I saw his sores mending right before my eyes—pus and scabs dissolving into skin resembling that of a newborn babe; nails quickening pink and translucent, and fingers suddenly becoming whole and agile.

I assure you, I would not have believed it had I not seen it myself.

Having known the leper before his disease overtook him—some nine years ago—I can attest to the fact that he was immediately and completely restored to the image of himself that I had retained within my memory.

Not only the leper, but everyone within seeing distance stared in shock for a couple of minutes until suddenly, the healed man bolted to his feet and started jumping and leaping and praising the God of heaven, shouting at the top of his lungs, "I'm clean! I'm clean! Exalt the name of the God of Israel! I have been made whole!"

I admit to you that I have never seen a greater river of tears streaming down a man's face—obviously springing from an internal fount of joy. I had to cry myself, in view of the overwhelming emotion as I was witnessing it. This man had been a member of my synagogue years before, a man whom I loved and esteemed highly. I had never known what sin he had committed that landed him in such a despicable state, but I have held him in appropriate contempt, regardless of my prior devotion.

The rabbi watched him with a look of delight for several

minutes before laying a hand on his shoulder to quiet him.
He then did a most peculiar thing—he issued a stern word of
instruction to the healed man involving two admonitions. First,
he forbade him to tell anyone about the incident—marvelous as it
was; and secondly, he commanded him to fulfill his obligation to
the Law by showing himself to the priest and subjecting himself to
a ceremonial proclamation of cleanliness.

He in whose possession this parchment has been carried
to Jerusalem is the same who was the leper and now is whole. I
witness to the healing with my own hand and feel it necessary to
send a detailed account of the event since there has never been
a leper healed in all of Israel, other than Miriam, who, as we all
know, was the sister of Moses, the prophet and miracle worker
of old.

Before I quit this correspondence, I need to ask clarification
concerning two issues—the very same two-sided injunction that
Jesus addressed with this man.

First, having received word from the Council alleging that this
Nazarene is trying to seduce all of Israel into believing that he is
the Messiah—thus securing their enlistment in his movement, or
rebellion—why do you suppose he would sternly forbid this man
to spread the news, as wondrous as this is?

Secondly, if he is a rebel as stated by the Council—acting
in complete disregard and open defiance of our most esteemed
traditions and laws—why would he, then, insist that this man go
directly to you to fulfill the requirement of the Law?

*I assume that you will send word quickly to apprise us
of the official position of the High Priesthood regarding these
issues, since we, the local synagogue rulers, lack experience in
offering alternative explanations for what appears to be obvious,
especially in light of the fact that the man was a confirmed
leper—whose healing now lends great credibility to the Healer as
owning a reputation commensurate with a man authorized by
God to do mighty deeds.*

*And on a more personal note, could you please advise me
concerning my own weakness in resisting Jesus' message, Jesus'
compassion, and Jesus' power to heal?*

Sincerely,

Ravid

"Leper lover," Caiaphas muttered under his breath.

"What did you say?"

"Nothing." Caiaphas looked up from the letter. "Did you see
the man who brought the letter?"

"No, he was already gone, sir."

"I need a list of replacement candidates for Ravid of
Chorazin."

"Begging your pardon, sir, what has he done to deserve
replacement?"

"We can't have a soggy sentimentalist in a position of
responsibility—not when this Nazarene is stirring up trouble all
over Palestine."

"Soggy sentimentalist? He's simply asking for a response."

"He shouldn't have to ask! A man in his position ought to know how to handle these delicate situations."

"Lord Caiaphas, what *is* the official position?"

"Concerning what?"

"The miracles?"

"Have you forgotten that this is the same man who disrupted our temple bazaar during the Passover last year, causing our profits to dip lower than ever in the history of my dynasty?"

"What should we do?"

"Send a delegation—this troublemaker must be watched, and when we catch him in his subversive scheming, we'll put a quick end to him and his following."

"What if the miracles really are valid? Then what?"

"The Almighty would never endorse a common, uneducated man like the Nazarene who possesses no pedigree and no credentials. Trust me; we have all the sanctions of heaven behind us."

Even hearts once inclined toward the God of heaven are prone to the hardening effects of religious influence. The lust for mortal power can blind people's eyes to the wonder of God's power. But God's healing grace is so much greater. He is able to reach through the infectious filth of a sinner's stony heart and restore that person to wholeness—that is, if the individual understands that he or she is ill.

The Faith of Four Friends

Matthew 9:1 – 7; Mark 2:1 – 12;
Luke 5:17 – 25

"He's back!"

"Who?"

"The Rabbi with the power to heal."

"You mean Jesus of Nazareth?"

"Yes, who else?"

"Where is he staying?"

"At Simon Peter's house, as usual. Do you remember our plan?"

"Yes, but Zadok is not going to agree to this."

"Probably not, but he can't stop us. You go fetch Meir and Akiva. We'll meet at Zadok's," Jesse commanded, turning to leave. He glanced back, taking note of Eli's hesitation. "Hurry! We have no time to waste. Remember what happened last time?"

Eli remembered, alright. It had happened in the late summer. Nearly everyone in Capernaum had turned out at Peter's home seeking something from the newly acclaimed Rabbi. Yet it had marked the beginning of a terrible ordeal for Zadok, the lifelong friend of Eli and Jesse—an ordeal that had intensified through the ensuing months. Now here it was, early winter, and the Teacher had returned, at long last.

Obeying his friend's directive, Eli started toward Meir's shop, his mind reaching back to the events of that unforgettable day—that day in the synagogue …

"Jesse!" Eli had grabbed his friend's cloak. He could feel his hand trembling against the coarse fabric.

"I saw, I saw!" Jesse exclaimed, his eyes wide with wonder. "He cast the demon right out of that man!"

"What do you make of it?" Eli questioned him.

"I don't know what to think," Jesse stammered in response. "I've heard about him—word gets around, you know."

"So have I, but I wasn't expecting him to show up in our synagogue," Jesse stroked his adolescent beard, contemplating the meaning of Jesus' presence. "Why do you suppose he's here?"

"I don't know; it just doesn't make any sense. If he wanted to establish himself as a teacher and a miracle worker, why wouldn't he stay in Jerusalem?"

"I hear that the authorities are up in arms over his alleged disregard of Sabbath laws—healing and all."

"My father said he hasn't broken any of God's laws—just their interpretation of them. Papa claims they are upset over the fact that he disrupted their profits at Passover when he ran off all those thieving money changers."

"I guess the real issue is, what do *we* think about him?"

"I think he has power from on high, otherwise, how could he do these amazing things?"

"Where's Zadok? I want to get his opinion."

"I haven't seen him all morning."

After searching the area, Eli and Jesse determined that Zadok had already gone home.

Arriving at Zadok's dwelling, they shouted at his door,

requesting to enter.

"Come in, then!" Zadok shouted back.

"Brother, we missed you at synagogue this morning. Are you ill?" Jesse greeted him in an affectionate embrace.

"No, it's Luann … again."

"What is it this time?"

"It is an illness in her mind, that's all!" Zadok's patience had worn thin. After both of his parents had died of the fever last year, he was left to care for his younger sister. Luann had been frail and sickly her entire life, her condition putting great demands on the family's resources and energies. Zadok had always resented the attention that Luann required from their parents—particularly his doting father—and was weary of the yoke she had brought upon his life now that they were gone.

Eli moved across the small room to the cot where Luann lay. She was flushed from fever, and her breathing sounded dangerously shallow.

"Zadok, I'm afraid this illness isn't simply in her mind," he reported.

"Leave it to a man's friends to come and cheer him up!" Zadok stormed out the door and into the courtyard, swearing. "I'm fed up with her! Does she not care that I need to live a life outside of her constant demands?"

Jesse followed his friend out the door. Putting a hand on Zadok's shoulder, he ventured a suggestion. "Zadok, I have an idea!"

Zadok kicked a small pile of rocks, sending a spray of pebbles against the stone wall nearby.

"Remember that Rabbi I told you about—Jesus of Nazareth?" Jesse paused for a response. After a moment he continued, "He is here in Capernaum, and the rumor is, he can heal the sick!"

"Sure, he can!" Zadok's sarcasm was cutting. "Do you suppose he can work magic on Miriam's father, too? Get him to consent to my proposal for marriage?"

Zadok was still bitter over the old man's refusal for the hand of his beloved Miriam. Insisting that Luann's situation was "all that a young man can handle," her father had turned Zadok away without hesitation.

Eli emerged from the dwelling, a deep frown furrowing his brow. "Brothers, I believe Luann is near death. Should we send for someone?"

"I hope she *does* die!" Zadok whirled around to face the two young men.

Grabbing him by the shoulders, Jesse shook Zadok, trying to bring him to his senses: "Stop it! Not even a fool would utter such nonsense!"

"Easy for you to say, Jesse. You don't live with the girl."

Jesse let go of his grip and attempted to reason with Zadok. "Listen to me, my friend. I am sympathetic with your dilemma. That is the very reason that I want you to hear me out. Rabbi Jesus is here in town. As soon as the Sabbath is over, I say we carry Luann to the place where he is staying and see if he will heal her."

"Take your *hocus pocus* and go!" Zadok stooped to pick up a handful of small stones. He began to pelt them at his friends, shouting, "Off my property, both of you!"

Jesse and Eli trotted off, stewing over the situation.

Zadok stumbled out to a gnarled tree a few feet away, and climbing up into the fork of a large, sprawling limb, he fell asleep.

The next morning, Luann was dead.

It was Jesse who found her. Having returned to check on both of them, he staggered out of the dwelling, wailing. Zadok awoke from his drunken stupor—startled and disoriented—and fell out of the tree, twisting and breaking both of his legs.

Zadok, now crippled, could not forgive himself for his negligence. He simply wanted to die.

Zadok's friends had grown more and more concerned as the months passed.

"Meir," Eli said as he poked his head through the doorway at his friend's house.

"What is it, Eli?"

"I need your help. Hurry!"

Meir kissed his mother on the neck and, grabbing his cloak, rushed out the door and into the street. "Where are we going?"

"The Rabbi has returned."

"The Healer?"

"That's the one. Jesus, they call him."

"Seems to me that if this Rabbi had wanted to distinguish himself, he should have changed his name."

"And what name would be suitable, do you think?"

"Rabbi Ben Abram, or something, I guess. But Jesus! Everybody and his cousin is named Jesus." Meir reached a foot out to trip a little boy running by. Catching the child in his arms, he tickled him and tousled his hair. "Anyway, what does Rabbi Jesus have to do with us?"

"We're taking Zadok to him, remember?"

Meir stopped in his tracks.

Eli turned to face him, "What? Don't stop! Jesse has this all planned out, and besides, we don't know how long Jesus will be here this time."

"But you and I both know that Zadok won't consent to this."

"That's just the point, Meir. Don't you see? We're taking him whether he wants to go or not."

"Zadok doesn't want to get well, Eli. He is convinced that he deserves this punishment. And I'm not so sure he's wrong about that."

Eli glanced sideways at his friend. "I know what he thinks, but Zadok has had trouble with his thinking ever since his folks died. You, on the other hand, have no excuse for such confusion."

As they walked along in silence, Eli recalled earlier days. "Remember when Zadok was full of life and goodness—back when we were boys? He was always helping us out of some sort of predicament."

"Yeah, ever since his parents' death, he just hasn't been the same," Meir said.

"And who's to say that we would be any different, if one of us fell into a hardship such as his?"

"Put me down!" Zadok thrashed with his arms, swinging at Jesse from the mat that was dangling in the air among the four young men.

"Shut up, Zadok!" Jesse rebuked, grinning.

"Are you amused?" Eli puzzled, looking over at his comrade.

"Sort of." Jesse returned his look. "At least we've stirred his passions again. It's just good to see some life in him, don't you agree?"

"Well, yeah, now that you put it that way," Eli was still sulking over his swollen lip. Zadok had managed to land a stinging blow to Eli's face as the four of them were lifting him up from the ground inside his dwelling. The whole place smelled of urine and barley beer, a nauseating combination. "What a man won't do for his friends."

"Do you think he'll really do it?" Eli questioned in quiet tones as they walked facing forward, their hands behind them, tightly clasping Zadok's mat.

"Heal him, you mean?" Jesse cast a backward glance at Zadok, making certain he couldn't hear.

"Yes, considering …"

"Considering what?"

"Considering what he did—neglecting Luann and all."

"Eli, I've heard that this Rabbi hugs lepers and eats with prostitutes. No telling what vile things those people have done," Jesse whispered. "I realize that the day of Luann's death wasn't one of Zadok's finer moments, but there is a good man in there underneath all the cursing and the beer."

"You're right, there is."

"What in the—?" Jesse's eyes widened with shock as they crested the hill carrying the protesting paralytic on his cot. There were people everywhere—crowded inside Peter's house, outside in the courtyard, and flowing out into the street.

"What are we going to do?" Meir asked, panting from the climb.

"I don't know. Just give me a minute."

Zadok laughed, sneering at his friends. "Like I said, just take me back home and leave me to my misery."

Eli whispered to Jesse, "We've come all this way, we can't give up now. It might be our only chance."

"That's exactly how I feel, Eli," Jesse winked. "Just follow my lead; I have an idea."

Jesse nodded his head to indicate that they should move to the far west side of the crowd. Navigating their way through people, trees, and houses, they made their way to the stairway of a dwelling several doors down from Simon Peter's. No one noticed as they began to climb. No one but Zadok, that is.

"What nonsense is this, you fools? Put me down."

"Shut up, Zadok," Jesse said. "If we are any kind of fools, we're fools for loving you too much to leave you to your misery."

The four friends lugged their burden across the "road of the roofs." Suddenly the crowd noticed their progress toward Peter's house.

"Hey!" one man shouted. "What do you think you're doing up there?"

"You can't do that!" a woman screeched from her spot under a tree. "We've been here waiting this whole time."

Gently placing the mat upon the roof, the four men began to tear up the tiles.

"The authorities are in there!" another man yelled. "They won't approve of this."

Zadok's head snapped up, the look on his face fearful. "What authorities? You can't do this to me!"

Jesse glanced at Eli. It hadn't occurred to him, but sure enough, earlier that day he had seen the delegation from the local rabbinical college, as well as some scribes and Pharisees from Jerusalem. His curiosity had been stirred when he noticed them standing outside the synagogue, but he had forgotten it in all the excitement.

"What do you think?" Jesse looked at Eli. "They're not going to like this."

"What can we do about that?" Eli answered. "This could be Zadok's only chance."

They bent over the roof tiles and finished the job.

Beneath them, in the terrace, which opened to the courtyard, sat Jesus, surrounded by the religious leaders. Dust began falling, then small pieces of sod from the roof above. Suddenly, patches of sunlight were peeking through. Some of the men looked up, their faces aghast when they realized, *Someone is tearing up the roof!*

In one combined effort, the four men pulled up an entire section of tiles big enough to let Zadok through. As they peered down into the room below, they saw Jesus.

He was staring up at them. The look on his face took Jesse and Eli by surprise. He looked elated! His eyes were dancing in the light of the sun, his skin crinkling up at the corners of his mouth where his smile couldn't stretch any wider. Nodding in assent, as if agreeing with the impulse of their stubborn love, he waved his hands to lower the mat.

Gasps and whispers escaped from the people surrounding Jesus. They were visibly appalled as they stared at the bottom of an old, dirty cot coming through the roof, slowly descending into their midst. The imprint of a human form sagged at the center of the mat, and Jesus stood, reaching to receive the smelly mat into his steadying arms—safely depositing the burden as it landed.

There lay Zadok, staring like a frightened animal up into the face of the Rabbi.

It must have been something in the Healer's eyes that caused Zadok to relinquish his protest, his fiery temper melting at the look of love on the Teacher's face.

Jesus' gaze searched the lame man's heart for one deep, penetrating moment. Zadok felt as if the Rabbi's eyes were probing inside him—looking into his past—back to the day his little sister had died all alone, while he had been dozing in a drunken stupor on a tree limb outside.

He felt the Teacher look straight into the horror of having let his parents down—of having betrayed their trust, as well as the trust of the Almighty who had put Luann in his care to begin with. He had buried his integrity and his hope with his sister, and now this Rabbi was digging up the shameful grave.

"Don't be afraid, my child," Jesus spoke with reassurance and affection, as if Zadok had expressed his fear out loud.

If only he knew . . . Zadok saddened. *Then he would*

understand my fear.

"You're forgiven," Jesus continued.

Zadok felt tears sting his eyes. *What?*

Jesus nodded reassuringly. *"Everything* is forgiven," he reiterated.

Shifting nervously, the onlookers glanced about the room. *Blasphemy!* their hearts whispered in silent accusation.

Jesus sensed their antagonism—sensed also that there was a morbid delight mingled with it. This was just what they had been sent to confirm—the blasphemous proclamations of the Nazarene, claiming God as his Father, and more than his Father, his Abba. Now he had told this common sinner that his sins were forgiven, as if he knew the heart of God.

He had played right into their hands.

"Why do you harbor those thoughts in your heart?" Jesus looked directly into the eyes of a Pharisee sitting nearby.

"What things?" he feigned innocence.

"You question whether I have the authority to forgive sins."

"Teacher, no one can forgive sins but God alone."

"Let me ask you, then, which would be easier for me to say: 'You're forgiven,' or 'You can walk'?"

The men looked at each other, nodding in mutual agreement, then back at Jesus.

"I suppose it would be easier to say your sins are forgiven," the holy man responded. "Because who would ever know the difference?"

"You are correct," Jesus agreed. "But if I have the authority to heal his legs, then you should know that I have the authority to heal his soul, as well."

He turned to look again at Zadok. "Son, I'm telling you that you are healed, body and soul. Pick up your mat and walk out of here right now."

"But you don't understand what I've done—" Zadok started to explain.

"Trust me, I understand," Jesus assured him.

Zadok looked up through the ceiling tiles. Jesse and Eli were leaning so far into the room, it was a wonder they hadn't fallen in. With tears in his eyes, Zadok stood up from the cot and tried out his legs. Tears streamed down his face in rivers of gratitude.

He fell on his knees before Jesus, thanking him over and over. Jesus lifted him from the ground and patted him on both shoulders. Zadok rolled up his mat and ran out the door yelling up at the roof, "I can't believe this!"

No one knows the private pain that exists in the hearts of others. Those who place their confidence in religion often require that a sinner first become penitent and then—and only then—he may approach God. Jesus, on the other hand, first welcomes sinners; and in the embrace of his gracious love, the sinner truly repents.

Son Rise

Luke 7:11 – 17

"Master," Simon Peter approached Jesus just as he was reaching for a crippled child, drawing her up into his arms.

"Yes, Peter, what is it?" Jesus held her suspended in the air for a moment, smiling into her eyes, putting to rest her fear of strangers. The little girl reached out to touch his face, tracing the outline of his smile with her tiny fingertip. The crinkles at the corners of his eyes deepened. She smiled back.

"Some men came calling," Peter said.

Jesus lowered the child into the crook of his arm. She sat, as if enthroned in the bend of his elbow, resting her arm on his shoulder, twirling his hair with her hand.

"Where were they from?" he asked, brushing some bread crumbs from the little girl's chin.

"Nazareth."

The gentle Healer turned slightly and perched the little girl on the broad ledge of a stone fence standing as tall as his waist. He took her bare feet into his hands and wiggled her toes, making her giggle. "Who were they?" he asked.

"Two of them were your brothers," Peter answered.

Jesus bent over the girl's knees and examined her crippled condition carefully, pushing Peter's patience to the edge with his deliberation. He then wrapped his hands completely around the girl's joints, with his thumbs pressing gently on her kneecaps. Glancing up into the little one's eyes, he winked to assure her that he wouldn't hurt her. She grinned and patted the top of his head.

"*You're* my brother, Peter." Jesus glanced his way for a

moment and then turned back to the girl.

"They are your blood brothers, Rabbi." He tried to disguise the irritation in his voice.

"What did they want, brother?" Jesus resumed the discussion.

"They said your mother is worried about the trouble brewing in Jerusalem."

"My mother ..." his eyes swam in an unexpected rush of sentiment.

Peter waited in silence.

"What trouble?" Jesus asked.

"Your habit of healing on the Sabbath," Peter answered.

"You mean, like this?" Jesus' hands moved to massage the girl's feeble knees in that instant. He turned to see Peter's face, his eyes moist with emotion. "Peter, how can any man claim to know my Father, yet deny that he would relieve the suffering of these, his children, at *any* time?"

"I dunno," Peter shook his head, distracted by the joy on the child's face as she began to kick her legs with newfound strength until, finally, she landed a foot right in Jesus' rib cage.

"Ouch!" he yelped, laughing out loud. "How about you and I show your mama how strong those legs are!" Jesus lifted her off the wall, swinging her around one full turn, then standing her on her feet. She pranced for a minute, skipping around his robe, and then headed straight into her mother's tearful embrace.

"You know that I have to tend to my Father's business,

Peter." He looked now into Peter's eyes, studying his response. "It's understandable that it would take awhile for my earthly family to catch on. But they will … eventually."

"Your brothers are troubled by the idea that you might be a prophet," Peter added.

"Troubled because *they* think I'm a prophet, or troubled because *others* perceive me to be a prophet?"

"Whatever the case, they want you to accompany them back to Nazareth and stop what you are doing."

"You know I can't do that, Peter." Jesus shook his head mournfully. "There are too many who haven't heard the good news. I can't be delayed in the interest of pointless discussions."

"So, what should we do?"

"We've finished here," he answered. "We need to be moving on."

Still making his way through Galilee, preaching, Jesus and his friends left Capernaum and headed south toward Nain. Thoughts of his mother stayed with him throughout the morning. He had spent thirty years in her gentle, nurturing presence. He loved her deeply, tenderly … with the love a man reserves only for his mother. He couldn't think of her without remembering the hearty smell of yeasty bread, the warmth of her gentle touch, the sound of her humming as she went about her daily chores, the way she tossed her head back when she laughed, and most significantly, the way she whispered in the night while praying.

Just as the sun was sliding into the horizon—just as the tiny town was coming into view—the travelers' ears perked up.

"Shhh ... listen," Jesus halted their progress. "What is that?"

"It sounds like flutes," Andrew answered. "And women wailing. There must be a burial procession headed this way."

The words no sooner left Andrew's lips than Jesus recognized the sound. It was a sound he had known since his childhood, having accompanied his mother to many funerals, including that of Joseph. He remembered the anguish he witnessed on his mother's face when he was laid to rest. A dark visitation had overshadowed their happy home and left his mother sobbing in widow's garb. He had sensed that her pain was deeper than she let on, and he had often heard her sobbing softly in the night. Ever since that time, death had mystified him. It was an unwelcome intruder from some unknown realm beyond sight.

Sure enough, these mourners were followed by a woman in widow's garments. It was clear by the look on her face that she was the one most tortured by this loss. However, her garments weren't new, so this wasn't her husband. Her mourning shroud was worn and faded. Jesus' sharp eye perceived that this was a widow grieving the loss of her child.

One of the villagers leading the procession stopped when he saw the travelers and the crowd trailing them.

"Shalom, brother," the man said as he approached with a somber countenance. "We beg you to let us pass freely since we are on our way to bury our dead."

"Who is it?" John asked, drawing nearer to the man.

"A poor widow of our city has lost her only child—her son. He took palsy and was cut short in his prime."

Jesus stepped forward, "A widow, you say?"

"Yes. Unfortunately, his death has left her without a provider. Her husband died years ago, back when the boy was a child."

"I see," Jesus nodded. He turned to the crowd, motioning them to remain where they were. "I need to have a word with the widow," he said to John.

He walked toward her, recalling in his mind the prophet Elijah, who had known a widow whose son had died. She had provided room and board for Elijah during a time of severe famine—though she'd barely had enough flour and oil to feed herself and her son. She had cried out to Elijah when the boy died, and Elijah had cried out to God on her behalf. God always listened to Elijah—a man submitted to his will—and it was no different on this occasion. The Lord had promptly raised the boy from the dead, though the widow was a Gentile, not from the people of Israel.

Jesus studied the widow, though she wasn't aware of him. Her head was bowed in sorrow, and she was stooped with the weight of grief. Crying shook her shoulders as if the earth beneath her were quaking.

Jesus fell in step with her, "Dear woman, don't cry," he said softly, as intimately as he would were he speaking to his own grieving mother. The tenderness in his voice betrayed the depth of his compassion.

She stopped, startled at the sound of his voice—a stranger approaching her like this in the moment of her greatest sorrow. "Were you speaking to me?"

"Please don't cry," Jesus entreated, reaching to touch her shoulder with a consoling hand.

Reaching with his other hand, he turned to stop the stretcher. Several gasps circulated in the crowd. Jesus looked at the men on whose shoulders it was resting, signaling his authority to do such a thing.

Why would he defile himself by touching the dead whom he does not know? They were perplexed.

"Young man," Jesus spoke loudly, looking at the dead man, as if summoning him from sleep. "Get up, and tend to your mother's tears."

The boy's eyes opened wide, as if startled awake. He sat bolt upright, sucking a dramatic draught of air into his lungs.

Some women screamed and fainted, while the four men dropped their burden, running from the sight of him. Jesus reached to grab the young man as the bier fell to the ground. Helping steady him to his feet, he reached at the same time for the mother's wrist, pulling them together, placing her hand inside of her son's.

The widow threw her arms around the boy, crying, "You're alive!"

"Mama, I don't understand."

She turned abruptly to face the Healer. Dropping to her knees in the dirt, she gripped Jesus' hand, pressing her lips hard against his knuckles. "Who are you? How can I thank you?" He felt hot tears running down the back of his hand.

Jesus pulled her to her feet, "Woman, my Father's ear is keenly attuned to the cry of a widow. Take your son home and rejoice."

He turned to face the mourners. A look of fear had swept over their faces.

"Surely we are in the presence of a great prophet," someone said.

"Just like in the days of Elijah," another voice shouted.

"He, too, raised a boy from death to life—the only son of a widow—just like we have seen here today!"

Jesus looked across the many faces and into the eyes of the man who said it. The man felt the searing penetration of Jesus' gaze. Jesus nodded at him, letting his own mind reach back to his brothers …

Turning back to the disciples, Jesus walked straight to John and said, "My mother is a widow, John. No matter what happens, you must see to it that she is never without a provider."

The God of heaven is deeply concerned over the welfare of his people. He acts through human agents to relieve the heartaches of those who grieve until the day that heaven will heal the breach completely.

Those who do not recognize his work voice their doubts loudly and without restraint. But those who do, continue gratefully—albeit somewhat quietly—through the journey of life.

The Champion
of Death and
Dying

Matthew 9:18 – 26; Mark 5:21 – 43;
Luke 8:40 – 56

Morning found the disciples huddled together in the boat, sleeping in a variety of positions. Just as the sun peeked over the cliff, Levi sat up to survey the sight. Laying his hand across the back of his neck, he rolled his head to work out the stiffness. His gaze involuntarily skimmed the tombs, still staring blankly from the limestone wall, but less intimidating in the dawn's fresh light. His eyes then traced the row of black caves to where they curved into an inlet and out of view.

Turning his gaze back to the boat, he caught sight of Jesus and the healed man sleeping in the stern, not ten feet from where Levi was sitting. Jesus was reclining against the edge, his head having fallen to rest on the crook of his elbow. The man, leaning against him, had rested his head on Jesus' shoulder. His face was clean now, even presentable. Levi wondered whether this might have been the first night's sleep he'd had in years. Tears stung his eyes when he realized that the mantle that covered the man was the Master's own—the fringes falling against the man's bare leg—shielding him from the chilly night air.

An hour later, the sun had risen and they had sent the man—fed, clothed, and restored to his dignity—back to civilization … back home. Jesus' final words commissioned him as a missionary: "Go tell your friends and family all that God has done for you."

As the disciples and the Teacher made their crossing back to Capernaum, the sun rose splendidly over a quiet basin of water.

The fickle sea now politely accommodated the fishing boat as it made its way back to its port, as if to offer a sullen penance for yesterday's upheaval.

Tired as they were, the men were greeted by yet another multitude of people. It seemed to Levi that it was a never-ending stream of broken humanity. And ever since the healing of the leper, the people were convinced that there was nothing outside of Jesus' power to cure and no sinner so vile that he could not approach the renegade Rabbi.

Strange, that though Jesus had raised a dead man to life just days ago, no one had yet ventured to ask that he repeat that miracle. It was almost unspeakable. In fact, it was unfathomable. Even to Levi. Troubling as it was to his mind, he realized that he still wasn't sure what he had witnessed.

"John," he hung back in the boat to ask the opinion of his colleague. Levi knew John to be a thinking man, deep and contemplative. Levi had observed his propensity to reason on many occasions, though he was a man of deep passions, as well.

"What's on your mind, Levi?" he answered without looking up from his work, securing the boat in safe harbor. Jesus had already debarked and made his way into the midst of the people, listening to their cries for help, wiping tears from their faces.

"Are we absolutely certain that the young man at Nain was dead?"

John's head snapped up, his gaze meeting Levi's. "What are you suggesting?"

"I'm just curious whether he might have been in a trance of some sort," Levi resisted the urge to squirm in the face of John's stern countenance. It was obvious his question wasn't sitting well with the fisherman.

"I think you might want to take that up with the Teacher," John advised soberly. "Sounds like you might be looking for more than a yes or no answer."

A strained silence passed between them before John straightened himself aright. He placed a hand on Levi's shoulder and said, "Look, brother. I know that there is more going on here than any of us bargained for. But don't start second-guessing Rabbi Jesus. Think about what you're seeing: He spends his days in the exhausting work of meeting people's deepest needs; he spends his nights in deliberate, intimate prayer with his *Abba*; he expends his wisdom teaching people a way of life that lifts their burdens instead of increasing them, a way that exalts them instead of depreciating them; and he causes evil spirits to flee from him every time he confronts them. Levi, he is delivering Israel from a great and terrible bondage. A self-imposed bondage, I'll give you that. But bondage of the worst sort ..."

Just then, a commotion stirred on shore, distracting John. "Well, will wonders never cease!"

A man was barging through the crowd, shoving people out of his way, shouting, "Let me pass—this is urgent!"

Falling on his knees at the Teacher's feet, he bowed his

forehead to the ground, right in front of Jesus, his fists grasping the long, woolen garment that descended to Jesus' ankles.

"Rabbi," his voice broke with emotion.

Levi stared in disbelief. "Is that who I think it is?"

John nodded in like amazement. "I believe it is!"

Jairus was one of the local elders who served as the leader of the synagogue. It was he who had asked Jesus to preach on that first Sabbath after he had joined his ranks. Jairus had come under no small amount of scrutiny by the Sanhedrin Council for what they considered an alarming lapse in judgment, seeing that the Nazarene had not been ordained by the rabbinical college, nor had he any other credentials in his possession.

Jairus was in the unfortunate position of risk—having to consider the possible loss of his status in synagogue as well as his clout with the religious rulers, yet wishing to remain in close proximity to this Teacher's message and power. Were he to confess, by word or deed, the leanings of his heart, he would be stripped of his authority and reduced to a man of common fare. He would, perhaps, even be put out of the synagogue for his failure to fulfill his responsibilities—banished from Israel's commonwealth.

"The man must be desperate, considering that he knows the official position of the Council concerning Jesus," John said out loud. "Let's go find out what's going on."

The two men climbed out of the boat and ran the short distance to where the Teacher had now bent to the ground in compassionate response.

"Master, help me, please," the dignitary sobbed.

"What is it, friend?" Jesus placed his hand on the man's shoulder. Jesus was never impressed, or lacking impression, when it came to a person's position or status.

"My little daughter—she is dying!" He wailed at the sound of his own words. "Please come and place your hands on her so that she might live!"

"Let's go," Jesus answered, helping the man to his feet. "Lead the way."

Stumbling forward, Jairus started back through the crowd. Jesus followed, along with his disciples. Curious onlookers fell into step, while others crowded around, trying to get his attention, trying to touch the Rabbi as if he housed some magical power.

There was one woman in the midst of that pressing throng who didn't wish to draw any attention to herself, lest she risk being put in her place. Ceremonially unclean because of a hemorrhaging condition, she was not fit to touch or be touched—most especially in the case of a rabbi, priest, or scribe.

Weak as she was from her condition, she kept pace with the movement, being pressed by the anxious crowd, until eventually, she found herself directly behind him, within arm's reach of his cloak. The fringes dangling from the corners of a Jewish man's cloak were the outermost article of his dress.

If she might just touch those mystical threads—those which represent the holiness of God as handed down to unholy men— perhaps it would not defile this holiest of men, but only pass on to her the blessing of God's love.

She reached, her spindly fingers grasping for hope. And just as she felt the tassels pass through her hand, she felt the illness pass from her body. Strength coursed through her veins with lightning speed. She was well!

Her weakness strangely absent, her defilement suddenly gone, she stood still from shock, letting the crowd swallow her into its midst. The tears spilling from her eyes seemed directly proportionate to the gratitude that was filling her heart. She was healed of her twelve-year plague—her banishment from Israel.

Suddenly, Jesus stopped. He wheeled around and surveyed

the throng. "Who touched me?" he asked.

Her eyes widened with recognition. *I've stolen a miracle!*

"Master," Peter stepped to his side. "Everyone is touching you. They're pressing in on you from every angle. What do you mean by asking who touched you?"

"I felt healing pass through me." His eyes continued to search.

Her conscience began to smart. *I've defiled the Holy One and delayed the healing of a rabbi's little girl.*

She rushed forward, out of the refuge of anonymity, falling with her face to the ground: "It was I! I only touched the fringes of your cloak, though, sir! I know I'm unfit for your audience, but I thought it wouldn't matter if I touched the threads of your mantle since they don't come into contact with the skin of your flesh."

Levi caught the self-deprecating tone of her words and knew precisely what she meant. She perceived herself *unfit* for this blessing. Hers was the same disposition as was the centurion's— that poverty of spirit that Jesus had said would be blessed. He watched Jesus' face with a familiar anticipation as the woman came forward to confess. First the scrutinizing look turned to recognition, then softened into compassion, and finally melted into outright pity. He stooped to the ground, resting his hand on the back of her head, as her face was now in the dirt. "Daughter," his voice was tender, entreating.

He moved to raise her up by her shoulders, helping her

to her knees. She looked into his face—the sound of his voice making it an irresistible temptation.

"Your faith has made you well. You may now go with the peace and confidence of knowing that *you* matter ... to me ... to the Father who healed you just now because you trusted him for it."

She collapsed into the Teacher's embrace, sobbing. How was she to be so honored that he should not only heal her, but rescue her from the condemnation of the rabbinical authorities, as well?

While his words of grace were yet falling upon her hearing, some men approached, coming from the house of Jairus.

"Don't bother the Teacher any further, sir," they said.

Jairus's eyes widened in fear. "Why? What are you saying?" He grabbed one of the men by the shoulders, demanding an answer.

"Your daughter died just minutes ago," he said, hesitantly.

"No!" Jairus's head fell back, his face inclined toward the heavens. "No-o-o-o-o!" he wailed.

"Come with us, sir," the servant took hold of his arm, steadying him against the emotional upheaval.

Jairus turned to Jesus, his face reflecting his shattered heart. "Why did you delay? We could have got there in time, if only you hadn't stopped for this wretched woman."

"Jairus," Jesus spoke with authority. "You can put the threat of death behind you now, for your worst fears have been realized. Unleash the faith with which you came, and press forward, believing."

"It's too late," Jairus sobbed.

"Peter, James, John," Jesus called the three of them. "Come with me, Levi," he looked over his shoulder to lay his eyes on the disciple. "Tend to this dear woman." He turned the other direction, saying, "Andrew and Philip, the rest of you tend to this multitude until we return."

Upon their arrival, the four men were greeted by a loud commotion—the sound of mourners. Familiar with these professionals—all actors—Jesus knew who they were and why they were there. They had got word that the little girl was on her deathbed. Hovering close by, like vultures, they were ready to descend upon the dwelling with a costly pretense of sympathy. Jairus was among the most prominent men of the city. Any professional would reason that he'd have provisions to pay handsomely for an impressive show of grief at his beloved daughter's funeral. Considering how deep Jairus's pockets were, the city would surely resonate with grief!

Besides, they would find a welcome there. The poor woman of the house, distraught with crying, would only find them a consolation. Let the pretenders voice her sorrow!

Jesus, accustomed to handling authentic heartache, had little time for this psuedosympathy. Looking one man directly in the eye, he confronted the loud show of emotion: "What's the commotion about? The child isn't dead, she's sleeping."

The man threw his head back scoffing, laughing Jesus to scorn. "This man doesn't know the difference between a dead girl and a child napping. Who does he think he is?" The remaining troop of mourners joined in the laughter.

Incensed at their disrespect, particularly in the face of the girl's grief-stricken father, James confronted them: "Explain to me how you can swing from utter despair to roaring laughter all in a moment!"

Silence fell over the room. Jesus showed them out the door, and taking Jairus and the girl's mother by the elbow, ushered the small assembly into the room where the little girl lay.

The cot in the center of the room was large, swallowing the small frame. The Healer walked to her side, studying his Father's handiwork. He reached to move a strand of hair from her face and with his finger followed the curvature of her cheek down to her chin, smiling at her innocence and beauty.

He took her hand in his and said, "Get up, little girl!"

Her mother gasped as the little girl opened her eyes, blinking back the rays of the sun, which bore down upon her through the only window in the room. Death's descent had taken her so deep into the darkness … so far from the light of the living.

"My baby!" Jairus sobbed. He fell prostrate before the Master, pressing his head to the ground at his feet. "How did I doubt you?"

"Your daughter is hungry," Jesus answered in consoling

tones. "She hasn't eaten in days."

The two men stood in the courtyard talking for several minutes. Jesus was aware of the precarious position in which the synagogue ruler found himself. "No one need know about this, Jairus. Just keep this to yourself."

When Jesus and the three disciples returned to the others, people pressed in for more healing favors. The disciples couldn't get a word in edgewise.

"Why didn't he allow us to go?" Levi finally inquired of John, his pride stinging with insult.

"Brother, do you remember the discussion we had in the boat just before this happened?"

"Yeah, I remember. So what?"

"Do you recall the question you raised about the dead man at Nain?" John pressed.

"You mean about the possibility of his being in a trance?"

"That's the one."

"Yeah, what of it?"

"There were people at Jairus's house who were scoffing at Jesus' power to raise the dead—professional mourners; you know the type. Death doesn't really affect them anymore; they are just there for the profit. Jesus must have sensed it before we got there."

"But what does that have to do with me?"

"Perhaps he was protecting you, Levi."

"From what?"

"From the influence of skeptics. After all, since the room was so small, only a handful of us could get in to witness what was going to happen. The rest of us would have had to stand outside with the scoffers."

"But why the three of you?"

"I suppose because we're too ignorant to know better. We don't have it all figured out, Levi. We just call it as we see it."

Levi was speechless. It was true, there would have only been room enough for a handful of observers, but he longed to have been among them. *Why is it so hard for me to believe?*

John started to walk away, but Levi stopped him. "Wait!"

"What is it, brother?"

"Why did he tell them she was just sleeping?"

"Maybe Jairus needed a little protection, too."

Even where faith is weak, the weak can be made whole.

The Withered Hand Made Whole

Matthew 12:1 – 14; Mark 2:23 – 3:6;
Luke 6:1 – 11

"Why do you wish to summon the Council?" the temple steward asked the petitioner. He didn't dare appear before the high priest without stating a reason.

"I stopped for the Sabbath in the region of Bethsaida, on the eastern shore of the sea, returning to Galilee from the Passover in Jerusalem. The renegade teacher from Nazareth was there, as well. Along with some other Pharisees, I witnessed another violation of the Sabbath ordinances. Inasmuch as we have been commissioned to report all unlawful activity committed by this pretender, I am here to execute my duty."

Within an hour, twenty-three members of the seventy-man Council were assembled in the hall, awaiting the report of the Galilean Pharisee.

Under normal circumstances, a Pharisee from the outlying regions would be considered among the lower classes of the astute. Jerusalem—being the center of religious activity and the hub of higher learning—produced the most reputable and the most highly esteemed scribes and Pharisees. However, several of the commoner class had stepped up, as of late, to assist in the acquisition of information that was being used to build a case against the carpenter-turned-rabbi from Nazareth.

The head of the Council rapped his staff on the floor: "This meeting has officially convened." Addressing the man from Galilee, he continued, "What charges do you bring before the Council today?"

"Shalom, most honorable brothers." The man made a slight

bowing gesture in homage to the ruling board of Israel. "As I explained to the temple steward, I was returning to Galilee from the Passover celebration and came upon Jesus of Nazareth in the region of Bethsaida, on the eastern shore of the Sea of Galilee."

The men in the room exchanged glances, their darkened faces pressing forward in order to catch the man's words as they fell from his lips, just like hungry beasts.

"Proceed," the ruler nodded.

"As I passed through a field on my way to the synagogue on the Sabbath, I witnessed his disciples harvesting corn."

Gasps rippled through the room.

"They were plucking, threshing, and rubbing the grains before eating them by the handfuls."

"Why would they do such a thing?"

"Obviously, they were hungry," he answered, a little taken aback by the question. He hastened to state an added assumption, "I guarantee you that their hands had not been ceremonially cleansed, either."

"Where was the Nazarene while this was going on?"

"He was walking with them through the field."

"We've heard rumors that he has miraculously fed thousands of people in desert places. Why not the twelve men he considers his closest friends?"

"That is precisely the question I posed to him."

"You confronted the violation, then?"

"Of course, I did. I asked him why he allowed it."

"How did he respond?"

"He said that our ancestor, King David, broke the Sabbath when he ate the bread from inside the tabernacle when his men were hungry; and, in fact, insisted that the temple priests break the Sabbath every week when they make the sacred loaves."

"He's shrewd, this Jesus," one of the scribes replied. "He has employed this kind of rationale on many occasions."

The ruler of the Council rapped his staff against the floor again. "We commend you for the faithful execution of your Pharisaical duties. You may be on your way."

"But," the man responded, wide-eyed, "that's not all."

"There's more?" the ruler's eyebrows arched high against his priestly cap.

"Oh, yes!" the Pharisee rubbed his hands together. "Once inside the synagogue, I took my place among the local dignitaries. The men had arranged for the attendance of a certain beggar named Chanan."

"You may forego any trifling details, such as names, and so forth," the temple steward whispered into the man's ear. "It wastes the precious time of the Councilmen and, well, it simply irritates them."

"The significance of his occupation relates to the nature of his illness," the Pharisee continued, a little miffed at the steward's advice. "He is known by everyone in the area because of his hideously deformed right hand."

"Why is that significant?" the high priest queried.

"He makes light of the curse of being left-handed by begging bread at the city gates with his disgusting right limb. The children in the region mimic his mannerisms as an affront to people they intend to insult. It is a widely known and despised situation."

"So, this man was in the synagogue that day?"

"Yes, but they had to pay him to come, because his deformed condition and his subsequent banishment from sacred places and society have caused his heart to grow cynical and calloused. He doesn't normally attend the synagogue."

"We don't really care about this sinner's heart," the ruler interrupted. "Just get to the point of your story."

"The Nazarene had been asked by the synagogue leader to preside that day," the Pharisee's tone reflected the insult he felt from the ruler's commentary. "Jesus noticed the man's hand right away. We all observed his gaze fall directly on it."

"So? What happened?"

"I spoke up and asked, 'If you think it is lawful to work by plucking grain on the Sabbath, do you think it is legal to work by healing on the Sabbath also?'"

"So, you put him on the spot publicly concerning the threshing issue?"

"Yes, but he didn't respond the way I intended."

"What do you mean?"

"He called the man with the wretched hand forward and

had him stand in front of everyone," the Pharisee elaborated. "The man played it to the hilt, as if he thought this whole scene was going to be very lucrative for him. He turned around and around, waving the vulgar thing in the air, causing the women to gasp." He paused, frowning. "You would have to see his hand to understand how offensive the thing actually is."

"Go on," the ruler waved his own hand as a gesture to keep moving.

"The Nazarene looked at me and posed the question, 'If you had one sheep and it fell into a well on the Sabbath, would you get to work and pull it out?' We all just looked at each other without a word. He appeared angry and answered the question himself with an edge in his voice, 'Of course, you would.'"

The Pharisee shifted his feet, appearing a little uncomfortable with the remainder of his task.

"Then he turned to the man who, by the way, was standing completely still by now, obviously a little concerned about the antagonistic feelings in the room. He said, 'Reach out your hand.'"

The Pharisee paused to look around the room. He knew the Councilmen wouldn't understand the significance of this moment if he didn't call attention to it, in spite of their insulting attempts to get rid of him.

"You see, that's what the people say to this beggar at the gate all the time. It has become a form of crude entertainment in that city. They approach the gate with bread or money and say,

'Reach out your hand.' They mean, of course, the horrid sight that they are paying to view. But this Jesus said it with a very authoritative tone in his voice, as if the hand was his to command."

"We understand," the old scribe nodded. "You intend to impress upon us that this Jesus was calling attention to their usual manner of speaking to the sinner."

"Thank you," he said feeling somewhat consoled. "And the man did."

The Pharisee suddenly felt all of the color leave his face. He felt a little lightheaded, as if by telling this, he was going to discredit himself.

"What's the matter with you?" the steward demanded, steadying the man with his hands.

"Well," he gulped. "It's just a little awkward to have to tell you that the man did just that, and as it stretched forward—right before our very eyes—the thing became as whole as my own hand. Restored like new!"

The room spontaneously broke into loud murmuring.

"Order!" the ruler shouted above the din, rapping his staff loudly against the wall this time. "You claim to have seen this restoration with your own eyes?"

"I did," he nodded.

"Are you here as a witness to this man's ability to work miracles?"

"No, sir!"

"What then?"

"To register an official report of unlawful conduct: This miracle was worked on the Sabbath!"

"Yes!" The ruler of the Council glanced at one of the more prominent members with whom he had argued earlier in the day. Then, looking back at the Pharisee, he said, "Duly noted. You are to be commended for the faithful execution of your duties. Well done!"

The prominent man on the Council cleared his throat loudly and stepped forward to speak. "Just a moment, please."

"Speak up, Nicodemus," the ruler said.

"If I might ask one question of this man," Nicodemus said.

"Of course," the ruler insisted, though somewhat sarcastically.

"Did the Rabbi from Nazareth touch the man?" Nicodemus asked.

"No, not exactly," the Galilean stammered.

"What do you mean, 'not exactly'?" Nicodemus demanded sternly. "Did he or didn't he?"

"No, he didn't."

"Did he speak a healing command?" Nicodemus pressed.

"No, he simply asked the beggar to reach out his hand," the man answered, "implying, naturally, that the hand should be stretched out in his direction."

"So, how can you be sure that he worked a miracle?"

"For heaven's sake! The man's hand was restored whole," the ruler interjected.

Nicodemus shot a look in his direction. "Then perhaps this was a work of God!"

"On the Holy Day!" the ruler stood up, his face filled with rage.

"Your Holiness," Nicodemus stood his ground. "Have you never seen rain fall on the Sabbath? Have you never witnessed the labor of a woman giving birth on the Sabbath? Have you never seen the bud of a flower open on the Sabbath? Or watched a ewe nurse her lamb?"

"What is your point?" the High Priest demanded.

"These are all silent works of God, executed in faithful rotation even upon the Sabbath, just as the sun rises and sets."

"Are you implying that the Almighty violates the Sabbath himself?"

"If you'll watch the sun make its descent this evening, I think you'll find the implications are his, not mine."

Beware of trying to put God in a box—no matter how sacred the box may be. As soon as you think you have succeeded, you will have, however unintentionally, placed yourself in the position of god of the box. And with this self-assigned authority over the box, you will deny God his sovereignty altogether, missing, as well, the wonder of his mighty deeds!

Healing in the Valley of Humiliation

Matthew 17:9 – 21; Mark 9:2 – 29;
Luke 9:37 – 43

Josias looked at his son, Lavan, lying in a heap in the corner of the room. He was sleeping peacefully for the moment. Josias sank down onto one of the small woven rugs across the room; from there he could watch over the boy until his mother returned from the market. For the past ten years, Kara and Josias had been watching over Lavan obsessively, fearful that if they took their eyes from him, they might lose him … forever.

It was during Lavan's fourth year that the visitation had come. The four-year-old child was outside the dwelling on a cloudy day, crouched down under a shrub, digging in the dirt with a sharp stick. Suddenly, he began shrieking in terror, rooted to the spot, unable to flee. Kara ran to his side and discovered that he had unearthed a small human skull. *Probably a journeyman's wife miscarried and buried the baby on the way*, Josias had reasoned.

Lavan was never the same. A spirit of evil found refuge in his terror and had been a tenant in his little body ever since. The boy seized regularly, often throwing himself into water or even into fire. The demon tortured Lavan with visions of horror and thoughts of self-destruction.

While in Jerusalem for the Passover, Josias had heard that there was a man in Palestine who was having amazing success over evil spirits. A distant cousin from Chorazin had witnessed with his own eyes the Rabbi's power to heal and drive out demons. With Lavan in his current condition, Josias was hungry to hear that someone might be able to help. And wonder of wonders, before leaving the holy city, Josias was informed that the Healer was in his home territory.

Ever since returning from Jerusalem, Josias had been busy searching into the whereabouts of this Rabbi. He had asked everyone at synagogue and even the Gentile merchants in the marketplace. Every report confirmed that Jesus had been seen in Caesarea Philippi, but the last sighting had been a week ago.

"Do you think he went north?" Josias asked the man selling leeks and cucumbers.

"That's what I heard," the man replied. "In fact, a couple of his disciples stopped by here looking for bread. I asked them where they were headed and one of them said they were on the way to Hermon."

"The mountain?"

"Yes. That's what he said."

Returning home, Josias spoke with his wife. "Kara, I'm taking Lavan north toward Mount Hermon in search of the Healer. Get some provisions together for our journey. It could take a day or two to locate him."

"What if you don't find him at all?"

"It can't hurt to try," Josias reasoned.

"His condition is worsening," Kara glanced over at the corner of the room where Lavan lay curled into the familiar infantile pose. "The seizures are coming more frequently, and I'm concerned about how you will get him home if the trip causes him to weaken."

"I'm just going to have to take my chances, my dear," he said as he touched her face with the back of his hand. She was still beautiful, though the strain of Lavan's condition had taken such a toll on her once youthful appearance. Brushing back a strand of hair that had fallen out of its knot, he continued. "Kara, he will eventually die if things continue as they are … we both know that. How can we afford to risk missing this opportunity?"

"You're right, Josias," she smiled, though only with her lips. Her eyes hadn't smiled in years.

"Josias!" Magen rushed into the dwelling, yelling.

"What is it?" Josias turned quickly. "You startled me, brother. I wish you could learn to enter the house more discreetly."

"There are some men here from Jerusalem. Teachers of the Law! Scribes!" As the youngest of the five brothers, Magen was always trying to impress Josias, the eldest. "I overheard them in the city gates asking if they could hire a Jewish man to serve as a guide to Mount Hermon."

"Whatever for?" he puzzled.

"They're in pursuit of the same Rabbi you're looking for," Magen's eyes danced. "I told them you would be happy to do the job."

"You what?" His eyes widened.

"Why not, Josias?" Magen persisted. "You'd be better off traveling with some other men anyway. In fact, I think I'll tag along."

Josias resisted the urge to inform Magen that he had been doing just that for the past twenty years—tagging along.

"I don't know whether that's a good idea," Josias's brow knit with concern.

"It's a marvelous idea," Kara interjected. "I would feel so much better about you having help with Lavan."

"Kara, I'm not so certain those are the kind of men who would help with Lavan," he scowled.

"But *I* will! Won't I, Lavan?" Magen moved to the corner of the room and crouched down to pat his nephew on the head. Lavan was still sleeping soundly.

"When do they want to head out?"

"They're waiting outside!" Magen leapt up and ran out through the doorway.

"Here," Kara gently shoved the satchel she had prepared while the discussion was underway. "Take good care of our boy." She reached up to pat her husband's cheek, tugging tenderly at his beard.

I hate to get her hopes up again, Josias thought as he lifted his son from the floor and into his arms. He could carry his small frame for the first few hundred paces, allowing him some time to wake up. *The last time we consulted a rabbi, Kara ended up crying for three weeks after the rabbi announced that the boy was beyond rescuing.*

"Shalom, brothers," Josias greeted the men as he walked out the door.

The next morning found the seven scribes arguing with nine of the Nazarene's disciples at the foot of Mount Hermon.

"Brothers," Josias interrupted. "I didn't come here to cause this kind of dissension."

"The dissension has nothing to do with you," one of the scribes shot back, putting him in his place. "These men are a bunch of manipulative liars, and we've finally caught them in their deception!"

Levi stepped forward, his facial muscles tense from the strain, "We aren't lying!" he shouted.

"Then go ahead, Tax Man," the scribe pointed a finger in his face. "Heal the lunatic!"

Josias winced. It still hurt to hear that word in association with his Lavan. He knelt to the ground, where his son lay twitching, and covered the boy's ears. He could never be sure what Lavan heard or understood.

"Look!" Magen yelled. "Is that the Healer coming now?"

Josias's head snapped around to see. Sure enough, there, coming off the mountain, were four men. One of them looked strangely radiant, as if his eyes were alight. Levi noticed it, too. Josias straightened himself and ran to greet them.

"Are you Jesus of Nazareth?" Josias inquired.

"I am," the Rabbi answered. "What's all this arguing about?"

"Sir, I brought my boy to you for healing," Josias began, his words tumbling from his lips in disorganized fashion. "He has had a demon most of his life—maybe even more than one.

The thing throws him to the ground, causing him to writhe and scream. He hits himself violently and foams at the mouth. We have sought help from so many, but his condition has only worsened over time. He can't even communicate any longer, as tormented as he is by this evil spirit."

"But why the argument?" Jesus persisted.

"I brought my son all this way for healing and when you weren't to be found, I asked your disciples to heal him."

"So …" Jesus looked intently at the man.

"They couldn't do it," he answered matter-of-factly.

Jesus sighed, shaking his head with disappointment. "Let me see him," Jesus ordered.

As they drew near, the crowd gathered around the boy. Jesus looked at Levi and Thomas with anguish in his eyes, "How long must I be with you before you will believe? Where is the faith you had just days ago?"

No one answered. The nine disciples just stood there, hanging their heads.

"How long has this been going on?" Jesus looked at the boy's father again.

"Ever since he was very small," Josias said. "The evil spirit throws him into fire and water—anything to try to kill him. Please help us, if you can," he pleaded.

"*If* I can?" Jesus answered. "What do you mean, *if* I can? Anything is possible for him who has faith."

"I believe!" Josias cried out, falling to his knees in front of

Jesus. "Please help my unbelief!"

Jesus laid his hand on the man's shoulder, sensing the burden his heart had borne for so many years. "Brother, you've suffered so much over your child. Cling tenaciously to the faith with which you came; it is enough."

Then, turning to face the boy, Jesus said, "You deaf and mute spirit, come out of the boy!"

The demon threw the youngster into a violent convulsion, and suddenly he was completely still.

"He's dead!" one of the scribes whispered.

"I think you're right," another man agreed.

Jesus bent to grasp the boy's hand, lifting him up from the ground.

"Son, your father wants to speak with you," Jesus said.

"Papa!" the boy cried, running into his father's arms.

Jesus glanced at Peter and nodded toward the city where there were headed.

"We must be on our way," Peter announced to the onlookers.

The thirteen men set out for Bethsaida, leaving the rest to depart by another route.

"Master," Levi sighed as he walked alongside Jesus. His heart was heavy with discouragement. "Why couldn't we cast the demon out of that boy?"

"You tell me, Levi." Jesus looked him in the eye. "Why couldn't you? You were casting demons out of people before John the Baptist was murdered. What has changed?"

"His death shook us up," Levi glanced away to avoid the Teacher's penetrating look. "You said that among all men ever born, none was greater than John."

"You're right, I did."

"So if he isn't safe, who is?"

"You must learn not to live in fear of those who can harm your physical existence, Levi," Jesus rested his hand upon his shoulder. "Only reverence him who has the ability to determine your eternal destiny."

"But how do you avoid such fear?" he asked.

"Expect trouble, then it won't cause you to question God," Jesus answered. "From now on, look at it this way: In this world you will have trouble, but there is no need to be afraid, for I have overcome the world."

"How can you say that? We keep waiting for you to overthrow Rome, but it doesn't appear that you're going to, much less overcome the whole world."

"Faith is the victory that overcomes the world, my friend," he smiled.

"So, what are you saying?"

"You didn't have enough faith to overcome the Evil One," Jesus answered. "If you have faith the size of a tiny mustard seed—the smallest seed in the garden—you could order mountains to move on the face of the earth—much more, demons."

"So, how do I maintain that kind of faith, Rabbi?" Levi pleaded.

"Talk to Abba." Jesus turned a glance to Peter, James, and John who had just been on the mountain with him praying. They had seen him clothed in radiance with the glory of God. "Pray to the Almighty Abba just as a child speaks to his father. He will answer more generously than you have asked. I give you my word."

When your faith fails you ... bend your knee, bow your head, lift your hands, and ask the Almighty Abba for aid.

"I Can See!"

John 9

"Davi, look!" Davina whispered in her brother's ear from behind him. The twins were standing in line in the temple court, waiting to drop their tithe into the trumpet-shaped boxes aligned by the wall. "Isn't he the man who's been begging at the temple gate all week?"

Davido glanced over his left shoulder, looking into Solomon's colonnade where a group of religious leaders had assembled to question the man.

"No, that's not the same man."

"How do you know?"

"The beggar is blind," Davido answered. "That man can see."

Davina punched her brother's arm, desperate to make her point. "I know! I know! But that's the man! I'm sure of it!"

"Don't be silly, Vina," Davido rubbed his arm, teasing her. "A blind man can't suddenly see. And stop hitting me, or you'll find yourself in a worse situation than that beggar."

Suddenly, a commotion caused the siblings to turn abruptly toward the columned hall. "Go get his parents!" one of the ruling priests yelled.

Davido gently pulled at his sister's cloak, moving toward the scene, hiding behind one of the columns.

"Look closely," Davina whispered. "Can't you see? It's the same man—I just know it."

"I see what you're saying. The shape of his face, the way his mouth sort of twists to one side when he talks. What was that he said to us when we were coming in?" Davido strained to recall his words.

"That's the point." Davina's eyes widened. "He wasn't there today. He's been there every other day, but not today."

"You noticed?" he looked back over his shoulder to catch the look on his sister's face.

"Well, yeah." She lowered her gaze, avoiding his eyes.

"I knew the purse was coming up a little short," he scolded gently.

"Davi, he's poor. He needed help," she whined.

"We tithe responsibly, Vina," he continued. "That's what we're doing now."

"It isn't the same, brother. We put our money in a box, but that just seems so far removed from the suffering of these unfortunate beggars. Besides, Papa would have done it."

"Papa …" Davido raised his gaze, looking off into his mind's eye. "You always have been more like Papa."

"And you, Davi," she tugged his beard a little too hard. "You have Mama's keen eyes and sharp tongue!"

Davido loved his sister's playful banter. "What *was* that phrase the beggar used?"

"He said, 'Gain merit by me!'" she said, thrusting her hand forward and staring blankly just past Davido's face and into the air.

"Stop!" He shook her by the shoulders. "I didn't ask for a reenactment, I just thought his choice of words was crafty."

Another commotion interrupted their discussion.

Two people were ushered into the colonnade, right alongside the once-blind beggar.

The presiding priest asked the couple, "Is this man your son?"

Davido edged nearer so he could hear.

"Yes," the man answered. "He is our son."

"Was he born blind?" the priest was stern.

"Yes, he was," the man replied, wringing his hands.

"How, then, can he see?" the priest shouted angrily.

"Sir," the woman raised her voice. "We know this is our son and we know that he was born blind, but we don't know how he can see or who the man was who healed him. He is old enough to speak for himself."

"They're afraid," Davido whispered to his sister.

"Afraid of what?" she asked, never taking her eyes off the trembling couple.

"Afraid they'll be put out of the synagogue," he frowned.

"How do you know?"

"Because, there's twenty-three of them out there, and that's the number of Council members needed to do an official excommunication."

"You mean, this is '*official*'?" Davina was shocked. "Are we witnesses to a real legal proceeding?"

"I guess you could say that," Davido answered skeptically. "Shhhh."

The father piped up again, "She's right. He's old enough to

speak for himself. Ask him."

The priest waved the two older people away. They scurried from the hall and out of the temple.

"Give glory to God, man!" the priest demanded. "We know this Jesus is a sinner."

"Look, whether he's a sinner or not, I can't say." The beggar had the upper hand, and having been treated so unkindly by the ruling class all his life, he spared them nothing now. "But a prophet, I assure you, he is!"

The Council members became restless, incensed at his suggestion. The lowliest prophet in Israel—visited by the Spirit of the Almighty—would be considered greater in authority than any priest or rabbi.

"Tell us precisely what he did," one of the Pharisees demanded. "How did he heal you?"

"I told you already," the man sneered. "He smoothed mud over my eyes, and when I washed it away, I could see.

Maybe you want to become his disciples, too."

"You filthy worm!" one of the rulers exclaimed. The Council broke out in cursing. "We are disciples of Moses, not of some *Galilean*. We know God spoke to Moses, but this *Nazarene*— bah! When did the voice from heaven ever speak to such scum?"

"Now this is strange!" The man was enjoying the spar. "He healed my eyes, and yet you know nothing about him. Since the beginning of time, no man has been able to open the eyes of someone born blind. Now you tell us that God doesn't listen to sinners, yet God listened to him! Considering that you know nothing about him—a man who bends God's ear—where does that put you?"

"Shut up!" the priest shouted. Turning to the temple steward he commanded him: "Get this man out of here. He's been nothing but a sinner since the day he was born."

The man dodged the steward and ran through the columns, toward Davido and Davina.

"Sir!" Davido said, as he brushed his shoulder in passing. "Shalom."

The man stopped and studied Davido's face. "Shalom, brother," he nodded.

"Is it true that you are seeing for the first time in your life?" Davido asked, struck with the intensity of his gaze.

"Yes."

"That must be amazing," he continued.

"You can't imagine!" he beamed.

"My sister and I saw the end of this confrontation," he said. "What caused the uproar?"

"It's the man who healed me," he answered.

"How did he do it?"

"He was walking into the temple with some other men—followers of his, I think, because I heard one of them ask him why I was born blind, as if I couldn't hear or feel. Men never stop to consider that we who are unsighted have extraordinary hearing. God is merciful, and he compensates for our lack of vision. Anyway, the man was questioning whether I sinned or my parents."

"I've met this Jesus," Davido said.

"You have?"

"Yeah," Davido glanced at his sister. "Anyway, how did he answer the question?"

"Truthfully and compassionately."

"What do you mean?" Davido pressed.

"He said, 'Neither.' "

"Really?" Davido puzzled. "What then?"

"He said that my suffering served a higher, moral purpose." Tears welled up in the man's eyes. "He told his friend that it was wrong to assign evildoing to any specific illness; some of us suffer from the fallen condition of the whole human race."

"You mean to imply that illness is a random effect of the fall of humanity?" Davido asked.

"That's what he said," the blind man nodded. "And he also

said that God would be glorified by my healing."

"Then what?"

"Then he squatted down beside me—I could hear him breathing. I heard him spit on the ground. The next thing I know, he said, 'Close your eyes, brother, or the light will blind you!' Then he put the clay that he had made with his spittle on my eyes."

"Isn't it wrong to make clay on the Sabbath?" Davido asked. "In fact, isn't it wrong to apply saliva to the eyes on the Sabbath?"

"That's why the Council is up in arms, brother." He glanced back at them. "If I were you, I'd be careful of falling in line with their thinking."

"What happened next?"

"He told me to go to Siloam and wash in the pool." The man made a scrubbing motion against his eyes. "The minute I did, I could see!"

"Just like that?"

"Just like that!"

"Nathan," a voice interrupted from behind the beggar.

"Jesus!" his eyes were wide with expression.

"Do you believe that the Messiah is the hope of mankind?" Jesus asked him.

"Who is he, sir, because I want to believe," the man answered eagerly.

"You have seen him with your eyes; now look at him with

your heart," Jesus smiled.

"Lord!" He fell at Jesus' feet. "I see you with my eyes and believe in you with all of my heart!"

Jesus bent over him in response. Glancing up at Davido, Jesus said, "I am the light of the world. I have come to give sight to the blind—those who think they see clearly, but actually walk in darkness."

One of the Pharisees who had spied Jesus talking with the man interrupted. "Are you saying that we are blind?"

"It would be better for you if you were blind—if you hadn't seen all the evidence you have seen," Jesus looked at him sadly. "Yet since your heart is so calloused, you see nothing at all."

The Lord doesn't measure us by the worst moment of our lives, but by the potential he has placed within us. Jesus heals, not on the basis of merit, but on the basis of grace.

Gratitude: God's Reign within the Heart

Luke 17:11 – 19

Davido hadn't been able to shake it off—the intuitive sensation that the Nazarene was the Messiah. After the healing of the blind man in Jerusalem, he stayed on the periphery of Jesus' itinerant followers, never allowing himself to participate in their conversations, but close enough to hear what was going on.

Davido knew that Jesus was aware of him. He often caught him looking intently across a sea of faces in the light of day, or across a desert fire at night. The tension behind Davido's eyes must have been obvious, and he wasn't the type to try to hide his feelings—never had been. It was the very reason he had had to send his beloved sister back home. She suffered so much anxiety over Davido's outbursts of emotion. Assuring her that he would return within a fortnight, Davido was glad to be rid of his concern over her while he was trying to sort out his feelings about Jesus.

He sensed the strain in those who had become disciples of the Master-Teacher. They had taken to the habit of glancing regularly over their shoulders as they walked the road toward Jerusalem. They hadn't wanted to attend the Passover this year, fearful that their Rabbi would be arrested by the High Council, and perhaps end as badly as Davido's own rabbi had—John, the wilderness Baptist.

He'd heard the rumors himself. They were circulating throughout Israel. Davido couldn't remember when his people had been so divided about anything—politics, personalities, or religious doctrine.

Ever since the raising of Lazarus—the deed that had sent the authorities into a decisive outrage—Jesus' fate seemed sealed.

From several paces behind, Davido noticed the strange company of men before Jesus' troop did. They were standing just beyond the city gate, beside some bushes. Dressed in the coarse sackcloth garments of lepers, they were hideous-looking creatures: hair matted into thick dreads, beards hanging in sickly yellow strands, fingers missing, faces pocked with sores and running with pus. Standing downwind, Davido could smell them even before he understood clearly what they were yelling.

"Jesus! Master, have mercy on us!" It wasn't that they weren't concerned with propriety; they simply couldn't run. They were missing the essentials that afford mobility: toes, soles, even whole feet. They were rooted to the spot with a few shrubs to shelter them from sun, wind, and rain. No telling how long they had been there.

Davido thought one of them looked a little odd. *They are all disfigured*, he reasoned within himself. *But that one, he almost looks like a Samaritan. No, it can't be. Even a leprous Jew wouldn't stand for such defilement as that.*

Jesus heard their cry. Halting his progress, he gazed over at the ten men. Davido saw the look of sorrow in his eyes. It was a look Davido had grown accustomed to seeing. He caught himself anticipating the look every time someone approached him for healing. It was like a shadow rising up from somewhere in his breast, crossing over his face, and moving him to respond.

Sometimes he was compelled to stoop and spit in the mud, sometimes to reach out and touch, and sometimes to wrap a leper into his embrace.

Davido had never seen a man look the way Jesus looked in those moments. It was a pained look … as if he were experiencing what he was seeing. It was difficult to describe and even more difficult to emulate. But he was trying. Something about this Rabbi was so real, so powerfully authentic, so riveting.

But this time, there was weariness on his face that served as the canvas of his compassion. Jesus was tired—bone tired. It had been this way ever since the news had filtered down to him that there was a warrant out for his arrest. The temple police were on official alert—he was not welcome in the holy city, especially in Abba's house.

Davido thought to himself, *I would be weary, too, if I couldn't go home.*

Jesus cupped his hands around his mouth and yelled to the men, "What do you need from me?"

"Mercy, Master!" one of them called back in a hoarse voice. "We are lepers."

Jesus stood silent for a moment, letting the echo of the man's voice finish its course. He looked at his twelve men. Then he cupped his hands around his mouth and shouted, "Go show yourselves to the priest."

They looked at each other with puzzled faces. Davido could hear them mumbling. Finally, they began to hobble off, one by one. A few steps into their journey, their hobbling was replaced with a solid gait. It wasn't but a minute later, the men were running to the city gates. Davido just stood gawking at the sight of them.

He turned to look at Jesus, who stood watching, smiling at the evidence of their restoration. Suddenly, one man stopped in his tracks. He turned back to look at Jesus. It was the Samaritan. He broke and ran as fast as he could, falling onto the ground at Jesus' feet, shouting, "Praise God, I'm healed!"

"Didn't I heal ten men?" Jesus bent over and helped him up, brushing him off while speaking to his disciples. "This foreigner doesn't really understand the significance of a Jewish priest, does he?" Humored at the irony, Jesus finished, "The nine men who live by the law are so bent on justifying themselves they may never look back to consider the wonder. Yet this man doesn't know any better than to obey the impulse of his heart and return to give glory to God!"

The words fell upon Davido's heart with a thud. He had never considered the connection. Jesus had been saying it all along: "The kingdom of God is within you. The reign of God exists within men's hearts."

Suddenly, in the sacred gratitude of this Samaritan, Davido could see what he meant. This man had obeyed the impulse of his heart—a heart where God was enthroned as King!

In that instant, Davido himself was healed of a blindness he had never detected.

Gratitude is the sacrifice most pleasing to the Healer.

The Last Lamp Lit

Mark 10:46–52

Just outside of Jericho, where the road was teeming with travelers, blind Bartimaeus sat begging. To him, the steady shuffling of feet signaled a meager hope that there would be bread before nightfall, as sighted men—moved by pity or guilt—occasionally tossed coins into his lap.

From time to time, the road grew congested and some careless sandal would stub Bartimaeus's toes, or kick a cloud of dust up into his face, causing him to retreat—choking and sputtering—swearing into the dark light of day. But the hunger gnawing at his belly soon scooted him near to the path again, full of anxiety; for the heavier the traffic, the lighter men's burden of conscience became.

Such was his dread that day when the faint roar of a crowd swelled into the blind man's ears. Bartimaeus reached out to grab a youth as he passed. "What's going on?" he demanded.

"Let go," the boy scolded. "Jesus of Nazareth is passing through."

Bartimaeus's darkened eyes widened. "Jesus!" he whispered. He had heard stories rumored about the Galilean. Rising to his feet and waving his arms above his head, he shouted toward the crowd, "Jesus! Son of David!"

"Shhh!" the youth commanded.

"Son of David!" he called again, louder. "Have mercy!"

Hearing his cry, Jesus slowed his step. Craning his neck, he searched the edge of the crowd.

A man moved to quiet Bartimaeus: "You have no right to interrupt …"

The familiar dagger of rejection penetrated the blind man's

heart as it had many times before. And suddenly, the crowd shifted, pushing him back, knocking him to his knees.

Just then—amidst the jeers of rejection—the voice of another sounded into his keen ears: "Bring him to me."

"You heard the man," the heckler said as he yanked at his cloak, "get up!" Bartimaeus staggered onto his feet.

Cautiously, he felt his way through the thicket of bodies, moving toward the voice, his hands coming to rest on Jesus. Hope surged in his chest as the Healer's hands enveloped his wrists.

Jesus asked, "What do you want me to do for you?"

Bartimaeus tightened his grip, and pressing near to his face, he implored, "I want to see ..."

"Very well," Jesus said without pause.

The words resonated into sudden awareness when without warning, Bartimaeus realized that for the first time in his life, he was staring ... into the eyes of compassion. "You can *see* ..." Jesus explained, smiling, "that your faith has healed you."

Blindness comes in many varieties: at times taking the form of tunnel vision stemming from a selfish heart; at others, an obstruction of sight due to stubbornness; perhaps surfacing as shortsightedness related to ignorance; or a shroud of darkness caused by depression or guilt. In the gospel of Mark, a plea from a sightless beggar, Bartimaeus, reveals the visual impairment of heartless people who leave compassion out of the picture. What a relief to discover that it isn't merely sight that Jesus offers the blind; it is a clear vision of the mercy of God.

The Mission Continues

Acts 3:1 – 16

"It's been three months since Messiah's death and resurrection, Peter," John said as they walked through the streets of Jerusalem. "When do you think he'll return to restore the kingdom?"

"I don't know, John," Peter answered. "Immediately after his ascension, I thought it might be any day. But ..." Peter's words tapered off as if he didn't quite know how to finish what he'd started.

"But ... what?" John pressed.

"Remember, he said that we would be his witnesses in Jerusalem, then in Judea, then to Samaria, and finally to the ends of the earth?"

"Do you think he meant for us to accomplish that before he restores the kingdom?"

"I'm beginning to wonder if that isn't *how* he intends to do it."

"Brother, you think he would leave it to *us* to accomplish a task of such magnitude?"

"I think he anointed us with his Spirit—every one of us—so that we could continue his mission."

"So, what's our strategy, if that's the case?"

"Same as his," Peter said.

The two men walked several paces in silence.

"Do you remember the day he told us that he does only what he sees the Father doing?" Peter resumed the discussion after considerable thought.

"Yeah, I remember." John was pensive. "He said that the

Father loved him and told him everything he was doing."

"Well, I think I finally understand what he meant," Peter continued.

"You do?" John stopped.

Peter turned to face him. "John, ever since the Spirit came, I have noticed something that I never noticed before."

"What is it?"

"In any situation, if I'll take pause—even ever so slight—I sense the impulse of the Spirit moving upon my heart."

"What do you mean?" John probed.

"It's as if the eyes of my heart open up and I can see what's really going on around me—what's really going on in the kingdom. My spirit intuits whether the Father is at work in every situation, and I sense the Spirit of Jesus calling me to get involved."

"Does this happen often?" John asked.

"More and more," Peter nodded. "But John …"

"Go on," John gestured with his hand for Peter to continue.

"It's risky," Peter looked intently into his eyes. "I'm not sure I'm comfortable with it yet."

"Peter… " John stroked his beard.

"What is it, brother?"

"I've sensed a similar calling, but I didn't know how to describe it."

The two men resumed their journey, approaching the

temple by way of the Beautiful Gate. It was three o'clock in the afternoon—time for the Jewish prayer service.

"Let us through, please," a man spoke.

Peter and John moved aside to make way for a man who was being carried by his friends. He had been lame since his birth. Peter and John recognized him immediately, for he sat beside the temple gate every day at about this time so he could beg alms from the people going inside for prayer. According to the rabbis, prayer and alms were inexorably tied. So, what better place for this poor beggar?

Immediately laying eyes on Peter and John, he held out his hand. "Brothers, the Holy One lavishes mercy upon those who show mercy."

Peter looked at him intently, studying his face, searching his eyes. When John saw the intensity of Peter's gaze, he, too, fastened his eyes on the man's face.

"Look at us!" Peter said.

Surprised by Peter's insistence, the man returned their look, thinking that a significant gift of money was coming his way.

"I don't have any money for you," Peter answered, as if the beggar had given voice to his anticipation.

"What is it, then?" the man asked, his eyes full of hope. Suddenly, recognition filled his eyes. "Wait!" his hand flew up, his finger pointing at Peter. "Aren't you the man who preached here on Pentecost?"

"Yes, did you hear?"

"I caught only fragments of what you were saying, there was so much commotion going on."

"I was telling the people the truth about the man who was crucified here just months ago—the Rabbi named Jesus."

"I heard about him." The beggar's eyes lit up. "My brothers brought me up here to beg for healing, but we missed our chance. He was already in captivity. That was the very day he died."

"Are you aware that he lives again?" Peter announced.

"I heard rumors. I didn't know what to believe," he confessed. "So, where is he, if that is true?"

"Seated beside the throne of God," Peter responded. "But he's coming back."

"What good is that to me?" The man hung his head, and disappointment filled his eyes. "If you have anything—bread or anything—I'd be grateful."

"I'll gladly give you what I have. In the name of Jesus Christ of Nazareth, get up and walk!"

The beggar's head snapped up to look again at Peter.

"What did you say?"

Peter reached for the man's wrist and gave him a gentle yank. Up he came, jumping! Ecstasy filled his countenance, and he started walking, leaping, and shouting, "Hallelujah!"

Peter and John watched him, smiling broadly at his joy.

"It's no wonder Messiah never rested from his work," Peter

said to John, still grinning at the man's antics. "How could you ever tire of giving people a second chance at living?"

The trumpet sounded one blast, signaling the people outside that prayer was about to begin.

"Quick," John said, ducking through the door and into the Temple courts.

The lame man ran after them, nudging himself between, holding tightly to their cloaks. Though temple decorum demanded silence during times of prayer, the man simply couldn't contain his joy. Spontaneous praise burst from his lips, and laughter rippled through the vast hall. Recognizing him as the lame beggar, people came rushing over to see. A look of astonishment filled the faces in the crowd.

"What happened?" someone demanded.

"Brothers and sisters," Peter shouted so that all could hear. "Why do you stand there looking at us as though we made this man walk by our own power or godliness? We are merely men, just as you are. The name of Jesus has healed this man!"

"But Jesus is dead!" one man shouted back.

"God raised him to life, and he has anointed us with his Spirit—all of us who are his followers—to continue his work."

On the day of his resurrection, Jesus told his followers in the Upper Room, "As the Father has sent me, so I send you." Jesus explained in detail what he was sent to do the first time he preached in the synagogue in Nazareth. Quoting the prophet Isaiah, he said, "The Spirit of the Sovereign Lord is upon me, because the Lord has appointed me to bring good news to the poor. He has sent me to comfort the brokenhearted and to announce that captives will be released and prisoners will be freed. He has sent me to tell those who mourn that the time of the Lord's favor has come ... "

Having completed his part in the mission, Jesus then passed it forward to those who trusted him as Messiah, Healer, Savior, and Lord. The anointing for mission came upon all believers on the day of Pentecost when the Spirit was poured out from heaven, and continues even still.

The healing grace of Jesus—once present in his person— continues through those who live in his presence.

Praise the LORD,
O my soul, and forget not
all his benefits—
who forgives all
your sins and heals
all your diseases.

Psalm 103:2–3

At Inspirio, we would love to hear
your stories and your feedback.
Please send your comments to us
by way of email at
icares@zondervan.com

inspirio

Attn: Inspirio Cares
5300 Patterson Avenue SE
Grand Rapids, MI 49530

If you would like further information
about Inspirio and the products we
create, please visit us at:
www.inspiriogifts.com

Thank you and God bless!